Constitutional LAW

eleventh
edition

STUDY GUIDE

Jacqueline R. Kanovitz

Michael I. Kanovitz

John C. Klotter Justice Administration Legal Series

Constitutional Law, Eleventh Edition
STUDY GUIDE

Copyright © 2005, 2008
Matthew Bender & Company, Inc., a member of the LexisNexis Group
Newark, NJ

Phone: 877-374-2919
Web site: www.lexisnexis.com/anderson/criminaljustice

LexisNexis and the Knowledge Burst logo are trademarks of Reed Elsevier Properties, Inc.
Anderson Publishing is a registered trademark of Anderson Publishing, a member of the LexisNexis Group.

This Study Guide was designed to be used in conjunction with *Constitutional Law*, Eleventh Edition. © 2008 by Matthew Bender & Company, Inc., a member of the LexisNexis Group.
(ISBN-10: 1-59345-502-X; ISBN-13: 978-1-59345-502-6)

Photocopying for distribution is prohibited.

Cover design by Tin Box Studio, Inc.

Editor   Elisabeth Roszmann Ebben
Acquisitions Editor   Michael C. Braswell

Preface

Coverage of the Student Study Guide

This study guide is designed to complement *Constitutional Law*, Eleventh Edition, by Jacqueline R. Kanovitz and Michael I. Kanovitz. It provides learning objectives, summarizes the main points, and contains a list of review questions for each chapter. The guide is not designed to serve as a substitute for the textbook. You will need to read the textbook in order to fully understand constitutional concepts, answer the review questions, and prepare for exams. .

Objectives to be Accomplished in the Course

This book is designed primarily for students considering law enforcement as a possible career choice. There are six main course objectives.

1. Students should acquire a general understanding of the structure and content of the United States Constitution. This includes knowledge of:
   a. the powers granted to the United States government,
   b. their separation among the President, Congress, and the Judiciary,
   c. the balance of power between the federal government and the states,
   d. the powers retained by the states,
   e. the content of the Bill of Rights, and
   f. Fourteenth Amendment limitations on the actions of state government.

2. Students should acquire an in-depth understanding of constitutional (and occasionally statutory) restrictions on the authority of the police to:
   a. investigate,
   b. interrogate,
   c. search for evidence,
   d. seize evidence,
   e. engage in wiretapping and electronic surveillance,
   f. detain for investigation,
   g. arrest,
   h. use force, and
   i. compel suspects to submit to procedures involving their bodies as a source of evidence against them (i.e., lineups, blood samples, etc.)

3. Students should also be able to apply the constitutional principles in these areas to routine fact situations.

4. Students should appreciate the serious consequences to the person affected, to themselves, and to the criminal justice system of violating the constitutional principles covered in this book.

5. Students should have a general understanding of the constitutional rights of the accused during the trial and post-trial punishment phases of the criminal justice process.

6. Students should be aware of how the constitutional principles discussed in earlier chapters apply to government employees (which they may someday be) in work-related disputes.

Contents

Briefing Cases

In order to understand more thoroughly how to locate court cases, to read cases for specific rules of law, and to understand how decisions of courts determine criminal justice policies and procedures, cases may be assigned for briefing and for presentation to the class as a whole.

In reading cases, look for the point of law being considered and read the case thoroughly, not only for that point, but for the reasoning of the court in reaching the decision on that point. After the case has been thoroughly studied, it should be "briefed." The form of the brief is generally the form of the sample brief below.

State the essential **facts** of the case briefly, but in sufficient detail to give the factual situation on which the decision was made. The **issue** is the question the court is called upon to decide. This, too, should be brief but clear. The **decision** is the holding of the court, and the **reasoning** of the court is the rationale of the judges in reaching their conclusions.

The **rule of law** is a brief digest of what the court held. This is the rule that must be followed by lower courts and justice personnel, until changed by court decision, statute, or constitutional amendment. A section of the Constitution is *not* a rule of law, nor is a statute or code provision (see the rule in the sample brief).

Use the sample brief on the following pages as a guide.

Sample Brief

SPINELLI v. UNITED STATES
393 U.S. 410, 89 S. Ct. 584 (1969)

Facts:

The defendant, William Spinelli, was charged with a violation of 18 U.S.C. Section 1952, which prohibits traveling in interstate commerce with intent to conduct a business enterprise involving gambling in violation of the state law. At the trial, he challenged the admissibility of evidence uncovered during the search of an apartment with a search warrant.

In the affidavit for the search warrant, the officer alleged that the defendant was observed crossing the bridge between Illinois and St. Louis on four occasions, and driving to the apartment house described; that the small apartment he occupied had two telephones with different numbers; that defendant was a known gambler; and that a confidential informant had advised that defendant "is operating a handbook and accepting wagers and disseminating wagering information by means of telephones . . ."

The evidence was admitted at trial in federal District Court, and the Court of Appeals sustained the warrant and affirmed the conviction. The U.S. Supreme Court granted certiorari.

Issue:

Was the informer's tip, as corroborated to the extent indicated in the affidavit, sufficient to provide a basis for a finding of probable cause to justify the issuance of a search warrant?

Decision of the Court:

The Supreme Court of the United States decided that there was not sufficient probable cause to justify the issuance of the search warrant. Reversed and remanded.

Reasoning of the Court:

The Supreme Court determined that the first three allegations were insufficient in themselves to justify a finding of probable cause. The Court said, however, as to the information from the confidential informant, "There can be no question that the last item mentioned detailing the informant's tip, has a fundamental place in this warrant application."

Referring to the case of *Aguilar v. Texas*, the Court held that the informer's tip was inadequate under the test stated in that case. The Court pointed out that the magistrate, in order to properly discharge his constitutional duty, must determine that probable cause exists and must make this determination from reliable information. If the probable cause is based on the informer's tip, the test enumerated in the *Aguilar* case must be applied. Here the Court said, "The tip does not contain a sufficient statement of the underlying circumstances from which the informer concluded that Spinelli was running a bookmaking operation."

In the concluding paragraph of the case, the Court, although denying that the tests were met in this case, reaffirmed the rule that an informer's information can be used to establish probable cause, if properly presented. In explaining the degree of evidence required for probable cause, the Court said, "In holding as we have done, we do not retreat from the established proposition that only the probability and not prima facie showing of criminal activity is the standard of probable cause."

Rule of Law:

Probable cause to support a search warrant can be satisfied by hearsay information; however, an affidavit for a search warrant must set forth sufficient underlying circumstances to enable the magistrate to judge the validity of the informer's conclusion, and the affiant-officers must support their claim that the informant was credible and his information reliable.

Dissent:

Justices Black, Fortas, and Stewart dissented. The dissenting judges felt that the warrant in the case was supported by a sufficient showing of probable cause and, therefore, the search should have been upheld. One of the dissenting judges explained that a police officer's affidavit should be entitled to a common sense valuation and should not be judged as an entry in an essay contest.

Chapter 1

History, Structure, and Content of the United States Constitution

Objectives

This chapter covers the events that led to the adoption of the U.S. Constitution, the structure and content of the Constitution, the limitations imposed by the Bill of Rights and the Fourteenth Amendment, and an overview of our judicial system, how cases reach the Supreme Court, and the remedies our legal system provides for police violations of constitutional rights. It is designed as an introductory chapter. The objectives of this chapter are to provide a working knowledge of:

1. The events that led to the adoption of the Constitution and Bill of Rights.

2. Major structural features of the Constitution, including the separation of the powers between the three branches of the federal government, the powers granted to the federal government, the nature of our federal union, and the sovereign powers reserved by the states.

3. Rights guaranteed by the first 10 amendments to the Constitution, known as the Bill of Rights.

4. Protections afforded by the Fourteenth Amendment due process and equal protection clauses.

5. Our judicial system and how cases raising constitutional questions reach the United States Supreme Court.

6. Why it is important for police to understand the Constitution and conform to its dictates.

7. Basic concepts that lay a foundation for the study of subjects covered in future chapters.

Discussion Outline

§§ 1.1–1.5   History of the United States Constitution

§ 1.6   Structure and Content of the Constitution

The original Constitution is divided into seven parts called "articles." The content of each article is as follows:

Article I. Establishes the legislative branch of government and lays out the powers vested in Congress.

Article II. Establishes the executive branch of government and sets forth the powers and duties of the President.

Article III. Establishes the judicial branch of government, outlines the jurisdiction of the Supreme Court and lower federal courts, and defines the crime of treason.

Article IV. Establishes the duties states owe one another, contains provisions for the admission of new states, grants Congress plenary power to govern territorial possessions of the United States, assures each state a republican form of government, and guarantees the states protection against external invasion, as well as federal assistance in quelling internal violence and uprisings.

Article V. Establishes procedures for amending the Constitution.

Article VI. Declares that the Constitution, laws, and treaties of the United States shall be the supreme law of the land and shall bind state judges, displacing contrary provisions in state constitutions and statutes, and requires that all legislative, executive, and judicial officers, both of the United States and of the individual states, take an oath of office to support the Constitution.

Article VII. Provides that the Constitution shall become effective when ratified by nine states and shall be operative in the states that ratify it.

§ 1.7   Separation of the Powers of the National Government

Articles I, II, and III separate the power of the national government into three branches—Legislative (which has the power to enact laws), the Executive (which is charged with enforcing the laws), and the Judiciary (which is charged with the duty of interpreting and applying the Constitution and laws of the United States in deciding cases and controversies). The first three articles describe the powers allocated to each branch. The Constitution forbids one branch from: (1) encroaching on the powers entrusted to another branch, and (2) delegating its power to another branch.

A. Encroachment

1. Congress may not exercise is legislative power so as to override Supreme Court interpretations of the Constitution. The power to interpret the Constitution belongs to the Judiciary. The Supreme Court is the highest authority on what the Constitution means and its decisions interpreting the Constitution become the law of the land. Unless the Supreme Court overrules a constitutional interpretation, a constitutional amendment changing the language of the Constitution is the only action that can eradicate it. Constitutional amendments must go through the procedure set out in Article V.

2. When the Supreme Court renders a statutory interpretation with which Congress disagrees, Congress can amend the statute. The amended statute will bind the courts in the decision of future cases. However, Congress cannot enact laws that change the outcome of cases that have already been decided. The judicial power includes the power to make binding dispositions of cases and controversies, subject to reversal only by a higher court.

B. Delegations of power to another branch. The doctrine of separation of powers also prohibits one branch from turning its powers over to another branch. Although Congress may not delegate responsibility for enacting laws to another branch, Congress may entrust rule-making authority to other branches provided it lays down clear standards to which the body exercising rule-making authority must conform.

§ 1.8   Nature of the Federal Union

The Constitution establishes a federal government with delegated and enumerated powers. The federal government can exercise only the powers that have been delegated to it. The division of power between the federal government and the states is accomplished through a combination of the following three sections.

A. Article I, Section 8, lists the powers that have been delegated to the federal government.

B. Article I, Section 10, withdraws certain powers from the states by forbidding them to exercise these powers.

C. The Tenth Amendment declares that all powers that have not been delegated to the federal government and that the states are not forbidden to exercise, remain in the states from whence the power originated.

§ 1.9   Powers Granted to the Federal Government

The Constitution establishes a federal government of expressly defined and enumerated powers. All laws enacted by Congress must be based on one or more of these powers because the federal government can exercise only the powers that have been delegated to it.

A. Expressly enumerated powers. Article I, Section 8, mentions and expressly delegates the following powers to the federal government:

- The power to levy taxes and make expenditures for the national defense and general welfare.
- The power to borrow money on the credit of the United States.
- The power to regulate interstate and foreign commerce.
- The power to establish national rules regarding immigration, naturalization, and bankruptcy.
- The power to coin money, regulate currency, and punish counterfeiting.
- The power to establish post offices and post roads.
- The power to secure for authors and inventors the exclusive right to writings and discoveries for a limited period.
- The power to establish judicial tribunals inferior to the Supreme Court.
- The power to make and enforce laws related to piracies and felonies committed on the high seas and offenses against the laws of nations.
- The power to declare war.
- The power to raise and support an army and navy and provide for their regulation.
- The power to organize a militia and call the militia into the service of the United States when necessary to execute federal law, suppress insurrections, and repel invasions.
- The power to govern the District of Columbia and all federal enclaves and establishments.

B. The commerce clause permits Congress to regulate three broad categories of activities: (1) the channels and instrumentalities involved in interstate commerce, such as interstate highways, railroads, airlines, and telephone and telegraph companies; (2) the movement of people and goods across state lines; and (3) commercial activity that has a close and substantial relationship to, or effect on, interstate commerce.

1. The reach of the third category, but not the first two, is limited to commercial activity. Congress, for example, can make transporting stolen motor vehicles across state lines a federal crime, even though this crime has nothing to do with commercial activity, because this measure is sustainable under the second category.

   a. *United States v. Lopez* — Part II

   b. *United States v. Morrison* — Part II

    C.   Implied powers. The powers granted to Congress are not restricted to the powers expressly enumerated above. The last clause of Article I, Section 8 grants Congress the "power to enact all laws necessary and proper for carrying into execution the foregoing powers." *McCulloch v. Maryland* — Part II.

§ 1.10   Powers the States are Forbidden to Exercise

Article I, Section 10, forbids the states from exercising the following powers:

- Enter into treaties, alliances, or confederations.
- Coin money, emit bills of credit, or make anything other than gold or silver coin legal tender in payment of debts.
- Lay duties on imports or exports without the consent of Congress.
- Keep troops or ships of war in times of peace.
- Pass any bill of attainder, *ex post facto* law, or law impairing the obligations of contract.

§ 1.11   Sovereign Powers Retained by the States

    A.   The powers retained by the states, called police powers, are ascertained by constitutional mathematics. Before the adoption of the Constitution, sovereignty resided in the states. The states yielded some of their sovereignty by delegating specifically enumerated powers to the federal government (§ 1.9). In addition, they agreed to specified restrictions on their own powers (§ 1.10). The powers retained by the states are determined by subtracting from their original sovereignty the powers they delegated to the federal government and the powers the Constitution forbids them from exercising. This method of fixing the boundaries between federal and state power is set out in the Tenth Amendment, which declares that "[t]he powers not delegated to the United States by the Constitution, nor prohibited by it to the States, are reserved to the States respectively, and to the people."

    B.   Because the states hold the residual of power (i.e., all powers that are not expressly delegated to the federal government and that the states are not forbidden to exercise), the powers retained by the states depend on the interpretation of the powers that have been delegated. There was a steady expansion of federal power at the expense of state sovereignty throughout most of the twentieth century. However, the tide has now turned and the Supreme Court has begun placing curbs designed to prevent Congress from using its delegated powers in ways that encroach on state sovereignty.

        1.   *United States v. Lopez* — Part II

    C.   While Congress has vast powers, its powers are mainly over the American people, not the states. Principles of federalism prohibit the federal government from using its Article I powers to regulate the actions of state governments in ways that infringe on their sovereignty.

       1.   *Printz v. United States* — Part II

    D. The federal government, nevertheless, does have powers that can be brought to bear directly on state governments. These powers are found primarily in the Fourteenth Amendment, which prohibits the states from denying individuals due process and equal protection of the laws and authorizes the federal government to enforce these limitations by appropriate legislation.

§ 1.12   The Bill of Rights

    A. Reasons for adopting the Bill of Rights

    B. Content of the Bill of Rights. See Figure 1.1 in the text.

§ 1.13   Applying the Bill of Rights to the States through the Fourteenth Amendment

    A. The Bill of Rights was initially binding only on the federal government.

    B. The Fourteenth Amendment, ratified after the Civil War, prohibited the states from depriving "any person of life, liberty or property without *due process of law.*" The main Bill of Rights guarantees have gradually been absorbed into the Fourteenth Amendment due process clause and made binding on the states through an approach known as "selective incorporation." The standard the Supreme Court has used to decide whether to incorporate a particular provision of the Bill of Rights into the Fourteenth Amendment is whether that guarantee is fundamental to the American system of justice.

    C. Incorporation into the Fourteenth Amendment due process clause means that states must provide at least as much protection as the U.S. Constitution requires. Federal standards become the minimum constitutional protection. States, however, remain free, pursuant to their own constitutions, to adopt a higher standard.

§ 1.14   The Fourteenth Amendment as a Limitation on State Power

    A. The Fourteenth Amendment regulates only the conduct of states and those who act under state authority; it does not regulate the conduct of the federal government or of private citizens.

    B. The Fourteenth Amendment contains two highly important limitations on the authority state governments to act: (1) the due process clause, and (2) the equal protection clause.

    C. The Fourteenth Amendment is phrased in the negative. It limits the authority of states to act; it does not impose affirmative duties on them.

       1.   *DeShaney v. Winnebago County Department of Social Services* — Part II.

§ 1.15   Due Process of Law

    A.   The Fourteenth Amendment due process clause reads "[n]o State shall . . . deprive any person of life, liberty, or property, without due process of law . . ." This language is the source of three different constitutional protections. The due process clause:

        1.   Makes most of the Bill of Rights applicable to the states (§ 1.13).

        2.   Requires state governments to use fair procedures in reaching decisions that deprive people of life, liberty, or property. This protection is called *procedural due process* (§ 1.15(A)).

        3.   Requires state governments to have an adequate justification or, in other words, a good enough reason for the deprivation. This protection is called *substantive due process* (§ 1.15(B)). The two main areas where the concept of substantive due process is used are:

            a.   Protection of "fundamental rights." The label of "fundamental right" has been reserved mainly for intimate, life-shaping decisions about personal and family matters, such as the right to marry, have children, direct their education and upbringing, terminate an unwanted pregnancy, forego life-sustaining treatment, etc.

                1.   *Lawrence v. Texas* — Part II

            b.   Protection against conscience-shocking conduct of public officials that is not otherwise prohibited by the Constitution.

§ 1.16   Equal Protection of the Laws

    A.   The Fourteenth Amendment equal protection clause forbids a state to "deny any person within its jurisdiction the equal protection of the laws."

    B.   In *Plessy v. Ferguson*, the Supreme Court interpreted the equal protection clause to permit state-mandated racial segregation as long as equal facilities were provided for members of both races. This position was overruled in *Brown v. Board of Education*. Since then, the equal protection clause has been interpreted to require the government to treat all persons who are similarly situated alike.

    C.   Whether laws that make distinctions between classes of citizens can withstand equal protection challenge depends on the review standard (called level of scrutiny) used to determine the regulation's constitutionality. Three different review standards are used: strict scrutiny (classifications based on race, color, religion, or national origin), intermediate scrutiny (classifications based on gender), and low-level scrutiny (classifications based on factors other than race, color, religion, national origin, or gender). The level of scrutiny generally determines the outcome; as a result, laws that make distinctions between classes of citizens based on race, color, religion, or national origin are rarely found to be constitutional.

D. The equal protection clause is also binding on police officers. Deliberately treating one person differently from the way the officer would another in the same situation because of the person's race, religion, gender, ethnicity, or sexual orientation is a denial of equal protection.

1. *Alexis v. McDonald's Restaurant* — Part II

§ 1.17 Adjudication of Constitutional Questions

The Supreme Court of the United States has discretion whether to hear a particular appeal. Requests to the Supreme Court for discretionary review are instituted by filing a petition for a *writ of certiorari*. Petitions for writs of certiorari brought by state prisoners reach the Supreme Court primarily through one of two routes—direct review and habeas corpus review.

A. Direct review. A defendant seeking *direct review* must appeal his or her conviction up the state appellate court ladder to the highest state court available before petitioning the Supreme Court to have his or her case heard on direct review.

B. Habeas corpus review. Federal law affords state prisoners a post-conviction remedy called *habeas corpus*. A state prisoner begins this action by filing a petition in federal court, alleging that he or she is being detained in prison in violation of his or her constitutional rights and requesting the issuance of a writ of habeas corpus. This procedure enables state prisoners to have a federal judge review the constitutionality of their state court convictions. If the prisoner's claim is denied by the federal district court, the prisoner may appeal to the United States Court of Appeals and, from there, the Supreme Court for discretionary (certiorari) review.

§ 1.18 Federal Remedies for Constitutional Abuses

Constitutional violations carry serious consequences—for the person whose rights are violated, the criminal justice system, and the officer personally. Constitutional misconduct can lead to:

A. Exclusion of evidence procured in violation of the Constitution.

B. Reversal of criminal convictions.

C. Disciplinary action by the police department.

D. Civil liability.

E. Criminal prosecution.

These sanctions are covered in later chapters, but are mentioned here to underscore the importance of the material that follows.

Review Questions

1. Why was the central government established under the Articles of Confederation unworkable? (§ 1.3)

2. When the newly drafted Constitution was submitted to the states for ratification, there were three major objections to its adoption. What were they? (§ 1.5)

3. How many articles does the Constitution of 1789 contain? In which of the various articles are the following provisions found? (§ 1.6)

     _____   a.   Procedures for amending the Constitution.

     _____   b.   Supremacy clause, declaring that the Constitution, laws, and treaties of the United States shall be the supreme law of the land.

     _____   c.   Powers of the President.

     _____   d.   Powers vested in Congress.

     _____   e.   Powers of the Judiciary.

     _____   f.   Requirement that all legislative, executive, and judicial officers, both of the United States and of the several states, take an oath of office to support the Constitution.

     _____   g.   Definition of the crime of treason.

     _____   h.   Duties states owe one another.

     _____   i.   Provision granting Congress the power to govern territorial possessions of the United States.

4. Which article or articles provide for the separation of powers between the three branches of the federal government? What is the main focus of the legislative power? The executive power? The judicial power? (§ 1.7)

5. What can Congress do if the Supreme Court hands down a decision interpreting the Constitution in a way that Congress considers wrong? (§ 1.7)

6. How does the Constitution spell out the division of powers between the federal government and the states? (§ 1.8)

7. List 13 expressly enumerated powers delegated to the United States Congress under Article I, Section 8. (§ 1.9)

8. Identify the three broad categories of activities that are within the regulatory reach of Congress under the commerce clause. Provide illustrations of the kinds of regulations that are permissible under each category. Which of these categories, if any, allows for regulation of noncommercial activities? (§ 1.9)

9. What is the constitutional basis for the "implied powers" of Congress? What do the implied powers permit Congress to do? (§ 1.9)

10. The Constitution not only enumerates the powers delegated to the federal government; it also specifically limits the powers of the states. What five powers does the Constitution prohibit state governments from exercising? (§ 1.10)

11. What is an ex post facto law? What is a bill of attainder? Which article prohibits ex post facto laws? Bills of attainder? (§ 1.10)

12. Which amendment reserves all powers that have not been delegated to the federal government and that the states are not forbidden to exercise to the states and the American people? (§ 1.11)

13. The Supreme Court has ruled that Congress may not use its Article I powers to regulate state governments in ways that encroach on their sovereignty. Give several examples of things Congress is forbidden to do. (§ 1.11)

14. When the first Congress met after the government was established under the Constitution, legislation was introduced to add a bill of rights. Why was this action necessary so early after the government was established? (§ 1.12)

15. In which of the first 10 Amendments is each of the following rights guaranteed? (§ 1.12)

_____   a.   Right to be indicted by a grand jury before being tried for a capital or otherwise infamous crime

_____   b.   Right to keep and bear arms

_____   c.   Protection against cruel and unusual punishment

_____   d.   Freedom of speech

_____   e.   Right to a speedy criminal trial

_____   f.   Protection against compulsory self-incrimination

_____   g.   Protection against unreasonable searches and seizures

_____   h.   Protection against the issuance of warrants without probable cause, supported by oath or affirmation, particularly describing the place to be searched or the persons or things to be seized

_____   i.   Protection against double jeopardy (i.e., being tried more than once for the same offense)

_____   j.   Right to a jury trial in criminal cases

_____   k.   Right to a jury trial in civil suits in which the amount in controversy exceeds $20.

_____   l.   Right to the assistance of counsel in criminal cases

_____   m.   Right to just compensation when private property is taken by the government for public use

16. All but three of the rights listed in Question 15 have been incorporated into the Fourteenth Amendment due process clause and made obligatory on the states. What test has the Supreme Court used to determine whether or not to incorporate a right? Which three rights, mentioned above, have not been incorporated? (§ 1.13)

17. The Fourteenth Amendment is the source of a number of different constitutional protections against the actions of state governments and their agents. Identify them. (§ 1.13, l.14, 1.15, 1.16)

18. Explain the difference between substantive due process and procedural due process. (§ 1.15)

19. State in one sentence what the equal protection clause requires. (§ 1.16)

20. Suppose John Doe, who is convicted of a felony in a state court, believes that his constitutional rights were violated. A person convicted of a state criminal offense whose federal constitutional rights were violated may succeed in having his or her case heard by the United States Supreme Court through one of two routes. What are these two routes? Trace the steps John Doe will have to take to reach the United States Supreme Court through each of these routes. (§ 1.17).

21. What five consequences may ensue from a police officer's violation of a citizen's constitutional rights? (§ 1.17)

Chapter 2
Freedom of Speech

Objectives

The focus of this chapter is on 10 words found in the first Amendment: "Congress shall make no law abridging the freedom of speech." These 10 words are extremely important to American citizens. The main goal of this chapter is to help students recognize when citizens are engaged in activity that falls within the purview of the First Amendment and, if so, to be thoroughly knowledgeable about when they may arrest citizens for what they *say* and when they may arrest citizens for what they *do*. To this end, students should emerge with an understanding of the following matters:

1. The broad range of activities regarded as "speech" under the First Amendment.

2. The extent to which legislatures are free to criminalize speech on particular topics. This, in turn, requires a thorough understanding of the five kinds of communications that are *not* protected by the First Amendment: (1) obscenity, (2) child pornography, (3) fighting words, (4) incitement to riot, and (5) threats.

3. The extent to which police officers are permitted to arrest people for *what* they say under disorderly conduct, breach of the peace, or similar statutes. This also requires a thorough understanding of the five kinds of communications that are not protected by the First Amendment.

4. The extent to which legislatures are free to enact laws regulating conduct associated with speech (such as parades, pickets, demonstrations, marches, handbilling, leafletting, etc.).

Discussion Outline

§2.1   Historical Background

A.   History of English repression

B.   First Amendment protects four freedoms:
     1.   speech,
     2.   press,
     3.   right of the people peaceably to assemble and petition the govern-
          ment for redress of grievances, and
     4.   freedom of religion.

C.   The First Amendment originally applied only to the federal government.
     Today, the First Amendment applies to all branches and levels of gov-
     ernment and all persons who act under the authority of the government
     (including police officers). The First Amendment, like all other portions
     of the Bill of Rights, applies only to the government. Conduct under-
     taken by a person acting in a purely private capacity is not restricted by
     the First Amendment.

D.   Importance of free speech in a democratic society

§2.2   Overview of Constitutional Protection for Speech and Expressive Conduct

The First Amendment prohibits the government and those acting under the
government's authority from *abridging freedom of speech.* When a citizen
claims that his or her First Amendment rights were violated, the court must
decide two questions:

A.   Was the claimant engaged in activity protected by the First Amend-
     ment? (§ 2.3)

B.   If so, did the officer's conduct abridge the claimant's *freedom of speech?*
     In answering the second question, a major difference exists in the First
     Amendment analysis between punishing speakers for *what they say* and
     punishing speakers for *what they do* (i.e., their conduct).

§2.3   Is Speech Involved?

The First Amendment concept of speech includes the right to:

A.   receive information,

B.   hold beliefs,

C.   communicate them to others by speaking; organizing and participating
     in parades, marches, pickets, and other public demonstrations; carrying

and displaying signs and placards; distributing literature, pamphlets, and other written materials; writing letters; soliciting funds and membership for organizations and signatures on petitions; broadcasting via radio, television, and cable; communicating via the Internet; bringing public interest litigation; participating in politically motivated business boycotts; engaging in artistic expression (i.e., dance, music, paintings), etc.,

D. engage in ideological silence, such as refusing to pledge allegiance to the American flag, and

E. engage in symbolic speech (i.e., mute conduct performed for the sake of communicating a message that is likely to be understood by others who view it).

§2.4   First Amendment Distinction between a Speaker's Message and the Conduct Associated with Its Communication

A. First Amendment protection for a speaker's conduct. People normally communicate by using spoken or written words. However, they sometimes engage in nonverbal conduct (marching on public streets, picketing in front of an abortion clinic) while communicating their message (chanting, carrying signs, passing out handbills). They may even engage in nonverbal conduct in lieu of words as a means of communicating their message (burning a draft card, wearing a black armband). Nonverbal conduct used as a medium of expression in lieu of words is called "symbolic speech."

B. *United States v. O'Brien* (a draft-card burning case) established the controlling test for when laws regulating conduct may be applied to persons engaged in speech. The Supreme Court held that *laws prohibiting conduct may be applied to persons engaged in speech when the law serves a substantial government interest that is unrelated to suppressing the speaker's message.* This rule applies whether the conduct accompanies, or is a substitute for, words (i.e., symbolic speech).

1. The general laws of the community (i.e., trespass, breach of the peace, disorderly conduct, blocking the public passage, etc.) may be applied to the *conduct* component of expressive activity when the law furthers an important government interest that is unrelated to suppressing the speaker's message.

2. *Texas v. Johnson*—Part II.

§2.5   Punishing Speech Because of the Content or Message

A. Legislatures may not enact laws prohibiting speech on a particular topic unless:

1. The speech falls within the small number of categories that have been excluded from First Amendment protection (i.e., obscenity, child pornography, fighting words, threats, or incitement to riot), or

2. The restriction advances a compelling government interest.

B. *Norwell v. City of Cincinnati*—Part II.

C. Rationale for excluding obscenity, child pornography, fighting words, threats, and incitement to riot from First Amendment protection: "Such utterances are no essential part of any exposition of ideas, and are of such slight social value as steps toward discovery of truth that any benefit derived from them is outweighed by society's interest in order and morality."

§2.6   Obscenity and Child Pornography

A. Obscene communications are not protected by the First Amendment.

B. The constitutional definition of obscenity was established in *Miller v. United States*. To be considered obscene in the constitutional sense, a literary work, taken as a whole, must:

1. appeal to the average person's prurient interests (i.e., arouse a shameful or morbid interest in sex),

2. describe or depict hard-core sexual conduct such as ultimate sexual acts (normal or perverted), masturbation, excretory functions, lewd exhibition of the genitals, or similar "hard core" sexual conduct that has been explicitly defined and banned by applicable law, and

3. not have serious literary, artistic, political, or scientific value.

C. States are not required to adhere to the *Miller* test when regulating child pornography. However, material is not child pornography unless it visually depicts real children engaging in sexual activities.

D. There are special rules governing obscenity searches and seizures.

§2.7   Fighting Words

    A. Communications amounting to "fighting words" are not protected by the First Amendment. *Chaplinsky v. New Hampshire.*

    B. The fighting words doctrine is limited to: (1) insults, (2) uttered in an individualized face-to-face encounter (language directed at a crowd will not suffice), (3) under circumstances that are, as a matter of common knowledge, inherently likely to provoke an immediate violent response. The third factor requires consideration of proximity and of the special characteristics of the addressee that affect the likelihood of a violent response.

        1. *Sandul v. Larion*—Part II.

    C. The requirement that insults be spoken under circumstances inherently likely to provoke the listener into retaliating with violence means that police should not arrest citizens solely for insulting them.

        1. *Buffkins v. City of Omaha*—Part II.

§2.8   Threats

    A. Threats are another class of speech that receive no protection under the First Amendment.

    B. To constitute a true threat, the speaker must communicate a serious expression of intent to commit an act of unlawful violence toward a particular person or group of persons.

        1. *Virginia v. Black*—Part II.

§2.9   Incitement to Riot

    A. The clear and present danger test, announced in *Schenck v. United States*, was the Supreme Court's first attempt to develop a test for when advocacy of violence ceases to be protected by the First Amendment. This test proved too malleable in times of national crisis and was used to prosecute harmless political dissidents.

    B. *Brandenburg v. Ohio* announced the present test: Speech advocating violence ceases to command First Amendment protection only when it is both: (1) directed toward inciting *immediate* lawless action, and (2) likely to incite *immediate* lawless action.

        1. *Hess v. Indiana*—Part II.

        2. Speech may not be suppressed out of premature fears of what might occur if the speech is allowed to take place.

3. When the threat of an outbreak stems from a hostile reaction to the speaker's views rather than premeditated incitement, peacekeeping efforts must be directed at the audience, not the speaker.

§2.10   Hate Speech

A. Hate speech refers to speech that expresses loathing for others because of their race, religion, ethnicity, sex, sexual orientation, or other vulnerable characteristics.

B. Hate speech is fully protected by the First Amendment so long as it remains an expressed belief and is not used under circumstances that amount to fighting words, threats of violence, or incitement to riot. Hate-motivated criminal conduct, in contrast, is not protected by the First Amendment.

§2.11   Crude and Vulgar Speech

A. Use of vulgar words in public may not be treated as grounds for arrest unless the words are used in a personally provocative fashion under circumstances that make them fighting words. The Supreme Court has on several occasions held that the "F-word" has constitutional protection. *Cohen v. California* (1971); *Hess v. Indiana*—Part I).

B. Crude and vulgar speech carries only limited protection and can be punished in certain contexts, such as in public schools.

§2.12   Commercial Speech

A. Commercial speech refers to speech designed to create interest in a commercial transaction. Commercial speech is the second type of speech that has been placed in the middle category.

§2.13   Restraints on Speech Based on Considerations Other than the Message

A. Many speech communication techniques, such as displaying outdoor posters and signs, distributing leaflets, door-to-door canvassing, soliciting contributions, and marching, picketing, and demonstrating involve speech intertwined with conduct.

B. Governments have greater authority to regulate a speaker's conduct than his or her message.

§2.14 Free Speech Access to Government Property: Public Forums and Nonpublic Forums

A. The constitutionality of restricting speech access to government property is determined through forum analysis. The court first classifies the location as being either a public forum or a nonpublic forum and then tests the restriction using the legal standards established for forums of that kind.

B. There are two kinds of forums—public forums and nonpublic forums.

1. Public forums include government locations that: (1) have a long-standing history and tradition of First Amendment use by members of the public, such as public streets, sidewalks and parks (called traditional public forums) or that (2) have been set aside for First Amendment use by members of the public, such as municipal auditoriums and public meeting halls (called public forums by designation).

2. Nonpublic forums include all remaining government facilities, such as public schools, courts, government office buildings, military installations, jails, police stations, municipal hospitals, municipal airports, and the like. This is the property the government uses to carry on the business of government.

C. Scope of regulatory control

1. Nonpublic forums. When the government acts as a proprietor regulating speech activity in nonpublic forums, restrictions on speech will be upheld as long as they are: (1) reasonable in light of the purpose served by the forum and (2) neutral as to viewpoint.

a. *International Society for Krishna Consciousness v. Lee*—Part II.

2. Public forums

a. Local governments restrict the time, place, or manner of using public forums for speech, provided the restriction: (1) is neutral as to content, (2) promotes a substantial governmental interest in restricting speech at that time or place or in that manner, and (3) leaves open ample alternative channels of communication. An ordinance that prohibits noisy demonstrations in front of schools during class hours is an example of a valid time, place, and manner restriction.

b. Laws that foreclose an entire medium of expression, such as ordinances that ban the display of residential yard signs or outlaw begging any place in the city, do not qualify as valid time, place, or manner restrictions, and violate the First Amendment.

       1.   *City of Ladue v. Gilleo*—Part II.

       2.   *Loper v. New York City Police Department*—Part II.

§2.15   Protecting the Community From Nuisances Linked to Speech

   A. Anti-noise ordinances

   B. Ordinances protecting residential privacy

   C. Anti-litter laws

   D. Interference with traffic and ingress and egress to buildings

   E. Restrictions on face-to-face solicitation

       1.   *International Society for Krishna Consciousness v. Lee*—Part II.

       2.   *Loper v. New York City Police Department*—Part II.

   F. Signs and billboards

       1.   *City of Ladue v. Gilleo*—Part II.

   G. Permit ordinances. To be constitutional, a permit ordinance must: (1) lay down narrow and objective standards for the permit grantor to apply, (2) not impose unreasonably long advance notice requirements, and (3) not include in the permit fee the anticipated cost of keeping hostile spectators in line.

§2.16   Free Speech Access to Private Property

   A. The First Amendment only limits the actions of the government.

   B. Private citizens, including corporate owners of shopping centers, are free to ban First Amendment activity on their property.

§2.17   Need for Precision in Regulating Speech

   A. Criminal laws that have the potential to be applied on a regular basis to persons engaged in speech must contain narrow, clear, and precise standards to guide arrest decisions.

       1.   Reasons behind this requirement.

       2.   There are three kinds of statutes that should never be used in a context involving speech, even when the speaker's conduct is not protected by the First Amendment.

     a.   Statutes authorizing arrests for "disturbing," "annoying," or "offensive" conduct.

        1.   *Norwell v. Cincinnati*—Part II.

     b.   Statutes authorizing arrests for refusal to obey a police officer's order to move on unless the statute contains objective, clear, and precise standards detailing when a police officer is authorized to issue an order to disperse.

     c.   Statutes authorizing arrests for "loitering."

§2.18   Summary and Practical Suggestions

Review Questions

1. What personal or social benefits does the constitutional guarantee of free speech promote? (§2.1)

2. What freedoms, in addition to freedom of speech, are mentioned in the First Amendment? (text of First Amendment)

3. "Speech" has an expansive definition for First Amendment purposes. List as many communicative endeavors involving "speech" as you can. (§2.3)

4. Define symbolic speech and give several examples. (§§2.3-2.4)

5. State the *O'Brien* test for when laws regulating conduct can be applied to persons engaged in speech. (§2.4)

6. Why did the Supreme Court find the Texas flag desecration statute unconstitutional in *Texas v. Johnson*? (§2.3)

7. The City of Misanthrope, fed up with homeless people sitting and lying on sidewalks, enacted an ordinance that prohibits sitting or lying on sidewalks in downtown commercial areas between 7:00 A.M. and 9:00 P.M. Sally, an advocate for the homeless, decided to protest the constitutionality of this statute by sitting on the sidewalk from 7:00 A.M. to 9:00 P.M., handing out leaflets announcing her protest of the ordinance. She was arrested for violating this statute. Does she have a defense under the First Amendment? (§§ 2.3, 2.15(E))

8. What speech topics have been excluded from First Amendment protection? (§§2.5-2.9).

9. What speech topics carry limited First Amendment protection? (§§ 2.5. 2.11, 2.12)

10. When, if ever, may police arrest citizens solely for what they say? (§§2.5-2.9)

11. State the legal definition of obscenity. What case established this test? (§2.6)

12. What is child pornography? (§2.6)

13. Why has the Supreme Court established special procedures for obscenity searches and seizures? What are they? (§2.6)

14. State the constitutional test for when language constitutes "fighting words?" (§2.7)

15. Why are insults and obscenities directed at police officers seldom treated as "fighting words"? (§2.7)

16. Although threats are not protected by the First Amendment, before a person can be punished for making a threat, a true threat must be made. What is a "true threat?" (§2.8)

17. When are police justified in arresting a speaker for advocating violence or other unlawful activity? (§2.9)

18. What is hate speech? When and to what extent is hate speech protected by the First Amendment? Discuss (§2.10)

19. When is burning a cross protected by the First Amendment? When is it punishable? (§§ 2.8, 2.10; *Virginia v. Black* (Part II)).

20. A police officer arrested a woman for shoplifting. As he was taking her into custody, she snarled at him: "You f——ing son of a bitch!" Can the officer charge her with disorderly conduct for using profanity? (§2.11)

21. What role does "forum analysis" play in First Amendment dispute resolution? (§2.13)

22. When are government-owned locations regarded as public forums? Provide examples. (§2.14)

23. When are government-owned locations treated as nonpublic forums? Provide examples. (§2.14)

24. What legal standard is used to determine the constitutionality of restrictions on speech in nonpublic forums? §2.14)

25. What legal standard is used to determine the constitutionality of restrictions on speech in public forums? (§2.14)

26. Classify each of the following locations as a public forum or a nonpublic forum and determine the validity of the speech regulation. (§§2.14-2.16).

a. An ordinance prohibiting begging in municipal bus stations? (Nonpublic forum/valid. *International Society for Krishna Consciousness v. Lee* (Part II))

b. An ordinance prohibiting begging anyplace in the city? (Public forum/ invalid. Laws that foreclose access to an entire medium of expression do not constitute reasonable time, place, and restrictions and violate the First Amendment. *Loper v. New York City Police Department* (Part II))

c. An ordinance prohibiting attachment of signs and posters to municipal lamp-posts and fire hydrants. (Nonpublic forum/valid)

d. An ordinance prohibiting excessively loud noises in front of churches and hospitals. (Public forum/valid "manner restriction" on speech)

e. An ordinance that prohibits display of signs within 500 feet of a foreign embassy that are critical of the foreign government. (Public forum/invalid. This ordinance cannot be sustained as a reasonable restriction on the location of speech because it regulates speech based on the content or, worse yet, on the viewpoint).

f. An ordinance requiring a permit to go door-to-door, soliciting contributions for any religious, political, charitable, or other cause. (Public forum/invalid)

g. An ordinance outlawing display of residential yard signs. (A person's front yard is neither a public forum nor a nonpublic forum. It's private property. In *City of Ladue v. Gilleo* (Part II), the Supreme Court determined that the heavy burden this ordinance placed on free speech rendered it unconstitutional.)

h. An anti-littering law forbidding distribution, by hand or otherwise, of leaflets or handbills on any city streets and sidewalks. (Public forum/invalid because it forecloses use of an entire medium of expression that is important to groups with limited funds)

i. An ordinance making it unlawful for persons canvassing, soliciting, or dis-tributing handbills to ring the doorbell of residences where "no solicitation" signs have been posted. (Public forum/valid "place restriction" on speech).

j. A parade permit ordinance that vests discretion in an administrator to refuse a permit when necessary to prevent "riots, disturbances or disorderly assem-blage." Public forum/invalid. Permit ordinances may not delegate discretion to consider the applicant's identity, message, or any assumptions or predic-tions as to the amount of hostility that may be aroused in the public by the content or message conveyed.)

28. What three conditions are necessary for a valid permit ordinance? (§2.15)

29. Why are shopping center proprietors free to ban picketing, handbilling, and other speech-related activities on shopping center streets and sidewalks in ways that municipal governments cannot? (§2.16)

30. Why are vague laws operating in a First Amendment context constitutionally objectionable? (§2.17)

31. There are three kinds of statutes that should never be used in a context involving speech, even when the speaker's conduct is not protected by the First Amend-ment. Identify them. (§2.17)

Chapter 3
Authority to Detain and Arrest; Use of Force

Objectives

Students should emerge from this chapter with a thorough grasp of the following:

1. The difference between voluntary investigative encounters, *Terry* stops, and arrests.

2. When police conduct constitutes a seizure.

3. The degree of suspicion needed for voluntary investigative encounters, *Terry* stops, arrests, weapons frisks, etc.

4. Amounts and types of information needed to satisfy the reasonable suspicion and probable cause standards.

5. Permissible and impermissible actions during *Terry* stops.

6. How to properly manage a pretextual traffic stop.

7. When the Fourth Amendment requires an arrest warrant.

8. What needs to go into a properly prepared affidavit in support of an arrest warrant.

9. How to execute an arrest warrant.

10. Prevailing patterns in state arrest law.

11. Fourth Amendment limits on the use of force, including deadly force.

12. The consequences of violating the Fourth Amendment.

Discussion Outline

§3.1   Introduction

     A.   The Fourth Amendment reads: "The right of the people to be secure in their persons, houses, papers, and effects, against unreasonable searches and seizures, shall not be violated, and no Warrants shall issue, but upon probable cause, supported by Oath or affirmation, and particularly describing the place to be searched, and the persons or things to be seized."

     B.   In order to be lawful, an arrest must comply with:

        1.   Fourth Amendment standards,

        2.   state constitutional standards, and

        3.   state arrest laws.

§3.2   Overview of the Fourth Amendment

     A.   An encounter between a police officer and a citizen implicates the Fourth Amendment only if the officer "seizes" the citizen. If there is no seizure (i.e., the encounter is con-sensual), police do not need justification for this contact.

     B.   The Fourth Amendment recognizes two types of seizures. They differ in scope, duration, and grounds for making the seizure.

        1.   An investigatory stop is a limited seizure made for purposes of investigation. It is permitted on reasonable suspicion of involvement in criminal activity.

        2.   An arrest is a full-blown seizure. It requires probable cause to believe that the per-son arrested committed a crime.

     C.   The Fourth Amendment is violated only if the seizure is *unreasonable*. A seizure may be considered *unreasonable* for any of the following reasons:

        1.   The police lacked adequate grounds for making the seizure.

        2.   The police failed to procure a warrant before making a nonconsensual entry into a private residence to arrest someone inside.

        3.   The police used excessive force to effect the seizure.

     D.   An unconstitutional seizure can:

        1.   Ruin an innocent person's reputation.

        2.   Destroy admissibility of evidence.

        3.   Lead to a civil suit and, in rare cases, criminal prosecution.

§3.3   Crossing the Boundary of the Fourth Amendment

There are three legally significant categories of police/suspect investigative encounters:

A. Voluntary investigative encounters

B. Investigatory stops

C. Arrests

§3.4   "Free Zone" for Investigative Work

A. Voluntary police/suspect investigative encounters are not regulated by the Fourth Amendment.

B. The hallmark of a voluntary investigative encounter is that police neither physically restrain the suspect nor behave in ways that would cause a reasonable person to not feel free to decline the officer's request, terminate the encounter, and leave.

1. *United States v. Drayton*—Part II.

C. No legally required level of suspicion is necessary to attempt to strike up a voluntary investigative encounter. Police may approach citizens and ask for identification, answers to questions, permission to search their belongings, consent to take a Breathalyzer test or accompany them to the police station, or for any other kinds of assistance in investigating the officer's suspicion of them. However, the suspect has a corresponding right to refuse the request.

D. Evidence secured through a suspect's voluntary cooperation is always admissible.

§3.5   "Seizure" Defined

A. A suspect is seized, within the meaning of the Fourth Amendment, when the suspect's freedom of movement is restrained and the suspect is brought under the officer's control, either through: (1) submission to a show of legal authority, or (2) physical means.

B. *Seizure by submission to a show of legal authority.* A show of authority occurs when police engage in conduct that would cause a reasonable person to believe that they are not free to ignore the officer's request, terminate the encounter, and leave.

1. Judges consider all the circumstances surrounding the encounter in applying this test.

2. The distinction between a voluntary investigative encounter and a seizure is one of degree. Relevant factors include the threatening presence of several officers, the display of a weapon by an officer, some physical touching of the suspect, the use of language or tone of voice indicating that compliance with the officer's request might be compelled, etc.

C. *Seizure by physical means.* If the suspect does not submit to the officer's show of legal authority, no seizure occurs until the suspect is actually brought under the officer's control.

1. *California v. Hodari D.*—Part II.

§3.6   Fourth Amendment Grounds for a Lawful Seizure

A. A correlation exists between the degree of suspicion warranted by what the officer knows and the type of action the Fourth Amendment allows the officer to take.

1. When an officer has nothing more than a hunch that a particular person is involved in criminal activity, the officer may investigate, but investigatory interactions must be voluntary; the suspect may not be seized.

2. Once the officer knows of and can point to specific facts that justify a *reasonable* suspicion that this person has committed, is committing, or is about to commit a crime, the officer now has constitutional authority to seize the suspect and detain him or her for investigation.

3. Once the officer knows of facts sufficient to warrant a reasonable person in *believing*, not just *suspecting*, that the subject is guilty of a crime, the officer may move in for an arrest.

B. Similarities between reasonable suspicion and probable cause.

1. Both involve assessments of the suspect's probable guilt.

2. Both may be drawn from the same sources of evidence. This evidence includes personal observations, physical evidence found at the scene, information supplied by other law enforcement officers or agencies or contained in police records, and reports from informants and ordinary citizens.

3. Judges use the same evaluation process for making both determinations. The evaluation process involves two steps. The judge first determines what the officer knew when he or she acted. Once the facts and circumstances known to the officer are identified, the

judge weighs these facts, along with rational inferences that arise from them, to decide whether the information known at the time of the action satisfied the relevant standard.

C. Difference between probable cause and reasonable suspicion.

- Probable cause requires a higher probability of guilt. The higher probability must be based on more evidence or more reliable evidence.

§3.7   Investigatory Stops

A. *Terry v. Ohio* is the seminal case that recognized investigative stops as a distinct category of limited seizures that are allowed on a lower degree of suspicion. The Court ruled that a police officer who observed three men engaged in what appeared to be the casing of a store had reasonable suspicion, justifying the officer in detaining the men for brief questioning and also in frisking them for weapons.

B. There are three constitutional requirements for a lawful *Terry* stop.

1. The officer must be able to point to objective facts and circumstances that would warrant a reasonable police officer in linking the detainee's conduct with possible criminal activity.

2. Officers must proceed with the investigation as expeditiously as possible to avoid unnecessarily prolonging the period of involuntary detention.

3. Officers must employ the least intrusive means of detention and investigation reasonable available that will achieve their goal.

§3.8   Reasonable Suspicion

A. In order to satisfy the reasonable suspicion standard, the officer must possess objective grounds for suspecting that the person detained has committed, is committing, or is about to commit a crime. To satisfy this standard, the officer must be able to point to specific facts that, taken together with rational inferences that arise from them, provide a rational basis for suspecting the detainee of criminal activity.

1. *Illinois v. Wardlow*—Part II.

B. Whether the facts known to the officer provide an objective basis for reasonable suspicion is determined from the vantage point of a trained police officer. Courts consider rational inferences that arise from the facts, as well as the facts themselves, in deciding whether the officer's information was sufficient to satisfy the reasonable suspicion standard.

1. Criminal profiles are groupings of behavioral characteristics commonly seen in a particular class of offenders. While police are entitled to take criminal profiles into consideration in evaluating what they observe, matches provide grounds for reasonable suspicion only if they serve to distinguish the suspect's behavior from the behavior one would ordinarily expect of a presumably innocent person in the vicinity.

2. Police officers may not act on information received from members of the public without independent corroboration unless they have a rational basis for believing this information appears to be reliable.

    Florida v. JL—Part II

3. An officer who makes an investigatory stop (or an arrest) at the direction of another police department or officer need not be informed of the evidence that supports the action. However, if the officer making the stop lacks grounds to support the action, the stop will be constitutional only if the department or officer requesting the action had grounds to support it or their combined knowledge supports the stop.

§3.9   Scope and Duration of Investigatory Stops

A. Investigatory stops are allowed on a lower degree of suspicion than arrests because they are designed to be less intrusive than arrests. When the police overstep the lawful boundaries of an investigatory stop, the stop automatically escalates into an arrest, resulting in a violation of the detainee's Fourth Amendment rights, unless probable cause for an arrest has already been established.

B. There are only two authorized activities police may pursue during an investigative stop. Police may: (1) take protective measures to secure their safety, and (2) investigate the circumstances that prompted the stop.

C. The measures an officer may take for his or her protection during an investigatory stop include the following:

    1. When the stop involves a motor vehicle, an officer may take the precautions covered in § 3.11 (C) (1) of this outline.

    2. Officers may frisk detainees for weapons only if they have reasonable suspicion that the detainee is armed and dangerous. A weapons frisk is limited to patting down the suspect's outer clothing. An officer may seize nondangerous contraband only if it is in plain view or is discovered by "plain feel" without exceeding the scope of the officer's protective weapons search authority.

D. The investigation must be conducted using the least intrusive and most expeditious means reasonably available. After a lawful *Terry* stop, the police have authority to perform the following when appropriate to investigating the underlying suspicion:

1. Ask for identification.

2. Question the suspect.

3. Communicate with others to verify the suspect's explanation.

4. Run a check of police records.

5. Fingerprint the suspect at the stop location when relevant.

6. Bring a drug detection dog to the stop location to examine the suspect's luggage, vehicle, or other property.

   United States v. Place—Part II *and Illinois v. Caballes*—Part II

7. Transport the suspect a short distance to a fresh crime scene for a showup identification.

8. Request *consent* for a full-scale search, a Breathalyzer test, or any other procedure that is designed to further the investigation.

E. Some investigatory techniques are too much like an arrest to be allowed on reasonable suspicion.

1. Police should *never* take the following actions until they have developed probable cause for arrest:

   a. Take detainees to the police station will for any purpose.

      Hayes v. Florida—Part II.

   b. Search detainees and/or their vehicles for contraband or criminal evidence without consent.

2. Police should also refrain from the following:

   a. Unnecessary display of weapons, use of handcuffs, etc.

   b. Unnecessarily moving the detainee to a second location.

F. A *Terry* stop must be: (1) brief (with 90 minutes probably being the outer limit), (2) conducted efficiently so as to avoid unnecessarily prolonging the period of involuntary detention, and (3) confined to investigating the suspicion that prompted the stop unless articulable grounds for reasonable suspicion of unrelated criminal activity develop during the stop.

1. *United States v. Place*—Part II.

§3.10   Traffic and Vehicle Stops

A. Stopping a motorist is *always* a seizure, whether the stop is made to check the motorist's license or vehicle registration, issue a traffic citation, or investigate suspicion of a non-traffic offense. Accordingly, probable cause is necessary to issue a traffic citation or make a traffic arrest, and reasonable suspicion is necessary to conduct an investigatory traffic stop.

- An exception exists for stops conducted at fixed checkpoints. Suspicionless checkpoint stops satisfy Fourth Amendment standards of reasonableness only if: (1) the checkpoint serves a special need beyond the normal need for crime control, (2) the decision to establish a checkpoint and the site selection is made by supervisory police officials, (3) the checkpoint is operated under standardized procedures that eliminate discretion in selecting which vehicle to stop, and (4) precautions are taken to minimize fear, danger, and inconvenience to motorists.

§3.11   Pretextual Traffic Stops

A. A pretextual traffic stop is a traffic stop made for an observed traffic violation in which the officer's real motive is to check out a hunch about unrelated criminal activity.

1. *Whren v. United States*—Part II.

B. *Grounds for a traffic stop.* Police need probable cause or reasonable suspicion of a traffic or equipment violation to make a traffic stop.

C. *Safety precautions during traffic stops.* Police may, as a matter of course: (1) order the motorist and passengers to remain outside the vehicle, (2) ask them whether they have guns or weapons, (3) visually look inside the vehicle and shine a flashlight around the interior, and (4) check for outstanding warrants and run a criminal records check.

D. *Scope and duration of traffic stops.* The dimensions of a lawful traffic stop are similar to a *Terry* stop. An officer conducting a routine traffic stop may request the driver's license, vehicle registration, and insurance papers, run a computer check on them, run a criminal records check, check for outstanding warrants, and ask a few general questions about the driver's destination and travel plans.

1. Questioning motorists about matters beyond the scope of the stop is permitted if it does not extend the duration. Such questioning may occur: (a) while waiting for the results of the computer run, and (b) while writing out a ticket or warning.

2. After this, the officer must return the motorist's documents and permit the motorist to proceed on his way unless: (1) reasonable suspicion of unrelated criminal activity has already arisen, or (2) the motorist consents to further questioning.

E. A consensual investigative encounter can follow a traffic stop without the motorist being expressly told that he or she is free to leave. However, the motorist's documents must be returned and the motorist must be asked in a courteous, nonthreatening manner if he would mind answering a few more questions before he departs.

1. *United States v. Alcaraz-Arellano*—Part II.

F. *Search authority during traffic stops.* Traffic arrests, even for minor, fine-only traffic violations, carry authority to search the motorist and passenger compartment of the vehicle for drugs, weapons, and evidence of any crime. Traffic citations, in contrast, carry no search authority.

1. *Illinois v. Caballes*—Part II.

G. *Racial targeting.* Deliberately treating one person differently from the way the officer would treat another in the same situation because of the person's race or ethnicity is a denial of equal protection of the laws (Fourteenth Amendment). Race and ethnicity may appropriately be considered in deciding whom to stop, frisk, search, etc., only when police have specific, trustworthy information to be on the lookout for a specific individual or individuals who are connected to a particular unlawful incident and who are identified in part by race or ethnicity.

Maryland State Conference of NAACP Branches v. Maryland State Police [Part II—Cases Accompanying Chapter 1].

§3.12 Fourth Amendment Requirements for a Constitutional Arrest

A. There are two kinds of arrests: (1) formal (i.e., intentional) arrests, and (2) de facto arrests, which occur when a seizure lasts too long or is too invasive to be allowed on reasonable suspicion.

B. The Fourth Amendment requires probable cause for an arrest.

1. Probable cause is determined based on the objective facts known to the officer at the time of the arrest. The test is whether the facts within the officer's knowledge would warrant a *reasonably prudent person* in the belief that an offense has been committed by the person to be arrested.

2. The probable cause that supports an arrest does not have to derive from the grounds used to make it. An arrest is valid if the objective facts known to the officer at the time of the arrest create probable cause to arrest the suspect for that or *any other* offense.

C. An arrest warrant is mandatory under the Fourth Amendment only when the police make a nonconsensual entry into a private residence to arrest someone inside.

   1. *Payton v. New York*—Part II.

D. An arrest warrant has two advantages over an arrest without a warrant. Good faith reliance on a facially valid warrant:

   1. Ensures that evidence seized during the arrest will be admissible.

   2. Immunizes the officer from civil suit.

E. Both advantages will be lost if the officer:

   1. deliberately or recklessly falsifies information in his or her affidavit in support of the warrant, or

   2. fails to include enough factual information to enable the magistrate to make an independent determination of whether probable cause exists for the arrest.

F. A defendant who is arrested without a warrant and not released on bail is entitled to a judicial determination of probable cause without undue delay after the arrest. Absent extraordinary circumstances, this determination must take place within 48 hours after a warrantless arrest.

§3.13   Probable Cause

A. An officer has probable cause to make an arrest whenever the totality of facts and circumstances known to the officer create a fair probability that a particular person is guilty of a crime.

B. Probable cause is analogous to reasonable suspicion in all ways but one—probable cause requires evidence that establishes a higher probability of guilt. Review §§3.6 and 3.8.

C. The Fourth Amendment requires probable cause for four different purposes: (1) an arrest, (2) an arrest warrant, (3) searches and seizures, and (4) search warrants.

   • Probable cause for an arrest and probable cause for a search or seizure differ only with respect to what the officer must have probable cause to believe.

§3.14   Requirements for a Valid Arrest Warrant

A. The Fourth Amendment warrant clause imposes the following three requirements for a constitutional arrest warrant:

1. The magistrate must make an independent determination that probable cause exists for the arrest.

2. The magistrate's determination must be supported by information given under oath.

3. The warrant must contain a particularized description of the person to be arrested.

B. A police officer begins the warrant process by preparing a sworn written statement, called an affidavit, in which the officer sets forth the facts on which his or her application is made. The magistrate reviews the officer's affidavit and decides whether the facts recited in it are sufficient to satisfy the probable cause standard. In making this determination, the magistrate considers both the content of the information and the reliability of the officer's sources.

1. Although the magistrate is responsible for making the probable cause determination, the officer is responsible for supplying enough information in his or her affidavit to enable the magistrate to make an independent decision.

2. The officer's affidavit must be given under oath and should have a certification showing this.

3. *United States v. King*—Part II.

C. Under the laws of most states, an arrest warrant must, in addition to the above:

1. Be issued in the name of the state or a municipality.

2. State the date when issued and the municipality or county where issued.

3. Designate the officer or class of officers who are directed to execute the warrant.

4. Command that the person described in the warrant be arrested and brought before the nearest accessible court for an initial appearance.

5. Describe the offense charged in general terms sufficient to apprise the party arrested of the nature of the charges.

6. Be signed by the judge of the court who issued it.

D. Even though the warrant has been properly issued, the arrest will not be valid unless the warrant is also properly executed. A lawful execution must, at minimum, comply with the following requirements:

1. The person executing the warrant must be the specific officer or a member of the class of officers to whom the warrant is directed.

2. The warrant must be executed within the territorial jurisdiction of the judicial officer who issued it.

3. The officer must present the arrest warrant or advise the person arrested that a warrant has been issued. If the person arrested asks to see the warrant, the officer must see to it that this occurs as soon as practicable after the arrest.

4. The officer must comply with the knock-and-announce requirement before making a forcibly entry into a private residence to arrest someone inside.

E. A valid arrest warrant issued in conformity with the requirements of the Fourth Amendment affords probable cause to arrest any person whom the police reasonably believe is the person named in the warrant.

§3.15   Arrests Inside a Private Residence

A. In the absence of exigent circumstances or consent, a warrant is necessary to make an arrest inside a private home.

Payton v. New York—Part II.

1. If the person to be arrested resides in the dwelling, an arrest warrant will suffice.

2. If the dwelling belongs to someone else, the police must obtain a search warrant as well as an arrest warrant.

3. Houses, apartments, hotel rooms, and motel rooms are considered private residences for purposes of this requirement.

B. In addition, police must knock and announce their identity and purpose before attempting a forcible entry into a private residence.

C. Compliance with the warrant and/or knock-and-announce requirement is excused if:

1. A person of sufficient age who resides on the premises grants permission for the police to enter.

2. Police have reason to believe that securing a warrant and/or complying with the knock and announce requirement will:

   a. endanger the lives or safety of the officer, the suspect, or a third party,

     b.   enable the suspect to escape, or

     c.   lead to the destruction of evidence.

3.   Police are in hot pursuit of a suspected felon encountered in a public place who flees and retreats inside a private dwelling.

§3.16   Use of Force in Making an Arrest or Other Seizure

A.   The Fourth Amendment prohibits excessive force in making arrests and other seizures. The standard used in Fourth Amendment cases is *objective reasonableness*. Police violate the Fourth Amendment when they use more force than a reasonable police officer on the scene would have considered necessary.

   1.   Factors considered in assessing whether the force was reasonable include the severity of the crime, whether the suspect posed an immediate threat to the safety of the officer or others, actively resisted arrest, or attempted to flee

   2.   Special rules exist for deadly force. Deadly force may be used only when an officer reasonably believes such force is necessary to protect self or others from serious bodily harm.

     a.   Police may shoot to kill when: (1) the suspect threatens the officer or someone else with a weapon; (2) the officer has probable cause to believe that the suspect committed or attempted to commit a crime involving serious bodily harm, deadly force is necessary to prevent his escape, and a warning is given, where feasible; (3) Police may not shoot to kill an unarmed suspect who has committed a nonviolent crime and is trying to escape on foot.

         Tennessee v. Garner—Part II.

     b.   Police may use vehicle contact or other maneuvers to end a high-speed chase that endangers the lives of innocent bystanders, even though their actions place the motorist at risk of death or serious injury.

         Scott v. Harris—Part II.

§3.17   State Arrest Laws

A.   The Fourth Amendment establishes the *minimum* requirements for a constitutional arrest. States remain free, as a matter of local law, to impose greater restrictions. A valid arrest requires compliance with more stringent requirements imposed by state law, as well as with the Fourth Amendment.

B. State arrest laws often distinguish between arrest for a felony (offense punishable by a prison term or death) and a misdemeanor (offense punishable by fine or jail sentence). An arrest for a misdemeanor generally requires a warrant unless the misdemeanor occurs in the officer's presence. To be committed "in the officer's presence," the officer must be aware that the misdemeanor is taking place while it is in progress.

§3.18   Territorial Limits on a Police Officer's Arrest Authority

A. *Intrastate limits on arrest authority.* A city or county police officer has no authority to take official action in other parts of the state unless:

1. state statutes confer this authority, or

2. the officer is in hot pursuit (i.e., immediate, uninterrupted pursuit of a person trying to avoid apprehension).

B. *Interstate limits on arrest authority.* A police officer's arrest authority ends at the state line. An officer may not take official action in another state unless statutes in the host state confer authority on out-of-state police officers to enter and perform the acts in question.

1. Most states have enacted *inter*state hot pursuit statutes, authorizing out-of-state police officers to enter the jurisdiction for purposes of making an arrest when the entry is made in hot pursuit. However, this authority is generally limited to felonies.

Review Questions

1. What besides compliance with the Fourth Amendment is necessary for a valid arrest? (§3.1)

2. An arrest may violate the Fourth Amendment for any of three different reasons. What are they? (§3.3, 3.5)

3. What negative consequences can ensue from violating the Fourth Amendment? (§3.3)

4. Three categories of police/suspect encounters were discussed in this chapter. Identify them. (§3.4)

5. How does a voluntary investigative encounter differ from the other two kinds of investigative encounters discussed in this chapter? (§3.4)

6. What level of suspicion is necessary for a voluntary investigative encounter? (§3.4)

7. What can police do if a suspect refuses to cooperate during a voluntary investigative encounter? (§3.4)

8. Define the term "seizure" and describe the two ways in which a seizure can be effected. (§3.5)

9. Why is it often necessary for courts to pinpoint the exact moment when a seizure occurs? (§3.5)

10. What test is used to determine whether a police officer's conduct constituted a "show of legal authority"? (§3.5)

11. What factors are relevant in applying this test? (§3.5)

12. Give several examples of seizures accomplished by submission to a show of legal authority. (§3.5)

13. What must police do to effect a seizure if the suspect does not submit to their show of legal authority? (§3.5)

14. What grounds are necessary for an investigative stop? For an arrest? (§3.6)

15. How are the reasonable suspicion and probable cause standards similar? How do they differ? (§3.6)

16. Describe the process courts use to determine whether police had reasonable suspicion for an investigative stop. Probable cause for arrest? (§3.6)

17. What was the first case to recognize investigative stops as a distinct category of seizures? (§3.7) What two rules did that case lay down? (§3.7)

18. What is the test for reasonable suspicion? (§3.8)

19. What is the difference between a hunch and reasonable suspicion? (§3.8)

20. What are the various sources of information from which reasonable suspicion may be drawn? (§§3.6, 3.8)

21. What is a "drug courier profile"? How are such profiles developed? What characteristics are included in this profile? For what purposes do police officers use such profiles? Does the fact that a suspect exhibits some of the characteristics listed in the drug courier profile guarantee that a court will find that the officer possessed reasonable suspicion? (§3.8)

22. When are tips from members of the public regarded as sufficiently reliable to stand on its own in providing reasonable suspicion for a *Terry* stop? When is corroboration necessary? (§3.8)

23. Why are police more restricted during *Terry* stops than after an arrest? (§§3.6, 3.9)

24. All activities undertaken during a *Terry* stop must be geared toward one of two general objectives. What are they? (§3.9)

25. When is a police officer allowed to frisk a detainee? What are the dimensions of a lawful frisk? (§3.9)

26. Under what circumstances, if ever, may police seize nondangerous contraband during a *Terry* stop? (§3.9)

27. What is the "plain feel" doctrine? (§3.9)

28. What investigative activities other than requests for identification and questioning are permitted during a *Terry* stop? What activities are not permitted? (§3.9)

29. What limitations exist on the duration of *Terry* stops? (§3.9)

30. What requirements does the Fourth Amendment impose for a valid checkpoint stop? What are some of the purposes for which checkpoints can be established? (§3.10)

31. What is a pretextual traffic stop? Are such stops legal? (§3.11)

32. What safety precautions are police allowed to take during traffic stops? What justification—probable cause, reasonable suspicion, or none—must police have in order to take each of them? (§3.11)

33. Under what circumstances may motorists stopped for a traffic violation be questioned about matters unrelated to the violation? (§ 3.11) Answer: (1) if the questioning does not delay completion of the stop, such as when it occurs while waiting for the results of the computer run or while writing out the ticket or warning, (2) when police acquire reasonable suspicion of unrelated criminal activity during the stop; and (3) if the motorist consents to remain after the stop is over.

34. Under what circumstances, if any, may police search a vehicle for drugs during a traffic stop? (§ 3.11) Answer: (1) when the motorist gives voluntary consent, and (2) when police make a lawful custodial arrest of a vehicle occupant for *any* offense, including a minor traffic or equipment violation. There are other grounds that the student will learn about in the next chapter.

35. Under what circumstances may police bring a drug detection dog to the scene of a traffic stop to perform a sniff? (§ 3.11) Answer: (1) when a sniff can be performed without delaying completion of the stop, or (2) when police acquire reasonable suspicion of drug activity during the stop.

36. What is necessary for a traffic stop to de-escalate into a voluntary investigative encounter? (§ 3.11)

37. What is the test for probable cause? (§§3.12, 3.13)

38. When does the Fourth Amendment require an arrest warrant? (§3.12)

39. What advantages accrue to officers from proceeding under an arrest warrant instead of making the probable cause determination on their own? (§3.12)

40. Under what circumstances will an arrest warrant be set aside and these advantages lost? (§3.12)

41. When is an arrestee entitled to a post-arrest judicial determination of probable cause? (§3.12)

42. Within what period after the arrest must it occur? (§3.12)

43. What three requirements does the text of the Fourth Amendment impose for a valid arrest warrant? (§3.14)

44. What is necessary to satisfy the Fourth Amendment requirement that an arrest warrant "particularly describe" the person to be seized? (§3.14)

45. What two Fourth Amendment requirements are generally necessary to arrest someone inside their own home? (§3.15)

46. What three Fourth Amendment requirements are generally necessary to arrest someone inside another person's home? (§3.15)

47. What locations are considered "homes" under the Fourth Amendment? (§3.15)

48. When are the police excused from complying with the requirements covered in Questions 45 and 46?

49. Who has the authority to give consent to enter a private home? (§3.15)

50. What constitutes "exigent circumstances"? (§3.15)

51. What test do courts use to determine whether the force used by an officer was excessive? (§3.16)

52 What factors do courts consider in applying that test? (§3.16)

53. What limitations does the Fourth Amendment impose on the use of deadly force? (§3.16)

54 List three situations in which resort to deadly force is permitted? List at least one situation in which it is definitely not permitted? (§3.16)

55. What requirements do state arrest laws normally impose for felony arrests? Misdemeanor arrests? (§3.17)

56. What is a felony? What is a misdemeanor? (§3.17)

57. When is a misdemeanor considered to have been committed in a police officer's presence? (§3.17)

Discussion Questions

Problem 1

At approximately 11:30 P.M. on January 4, 2005, the Whosville, Arkansas, Airport Drug Enforcement Agents received a phone call from the Los Angeles Airport Drug Enforcement Agents, who related the following information. A nervous-looking young man in a brown leather jacket and tan pants, traveling under the name John Roby, just purchased a one-way ticket for an overnight flight to Whosville with cash; he was carrying a briefcase, but no other luggage. Detectives North and South waited for the Los Angeles flight. Only one person fitting the description of Roby disembarked. The young man hurriedly left the airport and headed outside to the taxi area, unaware he was being followed. At that point, Detectives North and South approached the young man, identified themselves as DEA agents, and asked if they could talk to him. The young man, who appeared quite nervous, agreed. When the officers asked for identification, he produced a California driver's license issued to "John Roby." His hands were trembling. Detective North then asked Roby if he was carrying narcotics in his briefcase. When Roby said he was not, North requested permission to search Roby's briefcase, to which Roby responded: "Do I have any choice?" Detective North replied: "You have a right to say no. If you don't want us to look inside, we won't look inside. You're free to go on, but we'll need to detain your briefcase for a canine examination." Roby stayed with his briefcase. Three minutes later Detective East arrived with Rex, a trained narcotics detection dog. When the briefcase was put in front of Rex, Rex alerted. Roby was arrested for possession of drugs. The trial judge found that Roby's Fourth Amendment rights were violated at some point during this scenario and suppressed the evidence. When did the violation occur?

Problem 2

Officer Jones of the Rock Hill Police Department stopped Smith for driving 45 miles per hour in a 35 mile-per-hour zone. He informed Smith that he had been stopped for speeding and asked Smith for his driver's license and registration. As Smith handed him the documents, Jones noticed that Smith looked nervous and asked Smith to step out of his car and walk to the rear of the vehicle. He then asked Smith to place his hands on the trunk of the vehicle. As Officer Jones was conducting a pat-down for weapons, he felt a bulge in Smith's shirt pocket which, based on his prior experience, he instantly recognized as a bag of marijuana. Jones removed the bag from Smith's pocket and arrested him for possession of marijuana. Is the marijuana admissible?

Problem 3

Officer Quisart, acting on a hunch that Mary Wanna was transporting drugs, pulled her vehicle over for a seatbelt violation. While in the middle of writing out the ticket, he asked Mary whether she had drugs in her car, to which she replied "Frankly, that's none of your business." Hearing this, he stopped writing out the ticket, turned on a tape recorder, and for the next five minutes prodded her for information about her drug activity. She finally gave in and granted him permission to search her vehicle. Drugs were found in her trunk. Prior to her trial, she moved to suppress the drugs. Are the drugs admissible?

Problem 4

Officer Jones received a radio dispatch concerning a prowling complaint. According to the dispatch, the prowler was a white male youth wearing a black shirt and pants. He had been looking in the complaining party's window with a little flashlight. When he saw her, he took off running in a southerly direction. Two blocks south of the complaining party's home, Officer Jones spotted a white male youth in black clothing running through a parking lot. He intercepted the youth and arrested him for prowling, a misdemeanor under local law. After arresting him, Officer Jones performed a search and discovered a flashlight and some jewelry, later determined to have been stolen from a neighboring home. Is this evidence admissible?

Chapter 4
Search and Seizure

Objectives

This chapter completes the analysis of the Fourth Amendment begun in Chapter 3, which focused on limitations on the authority of the police to seize *persons*. Chapter 4 explores limitations on the authority of the police to *search persons, places, and things,* and to *seize things*. The student should leave this chapter with a thorough understanding of the following:

1. The historical reasons that led the Framers to limit the authority of the police to search for and seize evidence.

2. When police evidence-gathering involves neither a search nor a seizure and, accordingly, is "free zone" activity and, conversely, when it crosses the line and becomes a search (i.e., intrusion on a suspect's reasonable expectation of privacy) or a seizure (i.e., meaningful interference with a suspect's right to possession of property) and is regulated by the Fourth Amendment.

3. What the Fourth Amendment requires for a police officer to have authority to: (1) search for criminal evidence, (2) perform a limited weapons search, and (3) perform an inventory search.

4. The grounds for search authority, and the scope and intensity of search activity authorized for each of the various searches discussed in this chapter; namely, searches under the authority of a warrant, consent searches, searches incident to a lawful custodial arrest, exigent circumstances searches, motor vehicle searches, limited weapons searches, and inventory searches.

5. What the Fourth Amendment requires for police to have authority to seize property for each of the following purposes: (1) to use as criminal evidence, (2) to conduct a temporary investigation, (3) to preserve the status quo while applying for a search warrant, and (4) to impound the property.

6. How the requirements listed in items 3, 4, and 5 apply to: (1) searches of persons, (2) searches of vehicles, and (3) searches of premises.

7. The Fourth Amendment exclusionary rule and its various recognized exceptions.

Discussion Outline

§4.1   Overview of the Law of Search and Seizure

    A. The *Curious Case of the Artless Art Thief.*

    B. The Fourth Amendment is triggered only when police investigative activity constitutes either a "search" or a "seizure."

        1. A *search* occurs when the police intrude on a suspect's reasonable expectation of privacy.

        2. A *seizure* occurs when the police commit a meaningful interference with a suspect's possessory rights in property.

        3. Police evidence-gathering that intrudes on neither interest is not regulated by the Fourth Amendment.

§4.2   —Definition of a Search

The section defines a search and explores the boundaries between search and nonsearch activity.

    A. The Fourth Amendment was adopted in response to British search practices under general warrants and writs of assistance.

    B. Fourth Amendment Interpretation from *Olmstead to Katz.*

    The Supreme Court originally interpreted the term "search" as only protecting against physical intrusions into constitutionally protected locations (i.e., locations mentioned in the text of the Fourth Amendment). This interpretation left the police free to use wiretapping [*Olmstead v. United States* (Part II, Chapter 5)] and surveillance devices to gather private information about suspects as long as they did not trespass on the suspect's property. In *United States v. Katz*, the Supreme Court overruled Olmstead and established the contemporary definition of a search. [*Katz v. United States* (Part II, Chapter 5)].

    B. Search defined

    A *search* occurs when the police intrude on a suspect's reasonable expectation of privacy. A police invasion of privacy can be committed either by making a physical entry into a constitutionally protected location or through technological invasions of privacy.

        1. *Physical entry into constitutionally protected location.* The Fourth Amendment protects four broad categories of locations from unreasonable government intrusions: persons, houses, papers, and effects.

2.   *Use of police surveillance technologies to invade privacy.* Using devices to intercept private communications or to conduct surveillance of activities that take place inside a home also constitutes a search. This aspect of Fourth Amendment search law is covered in Chapter 5.

C.   Nonsearches ("free zone" activity)

The Fourth Amendment definition of a search has two components: (1) police activity and (2) an invasion of a suspect's reasonable expectation of privacy.

1.   Searches conducted by private parties without police involvement are not regulated by the Fourth Amendment. The Fourth Amendment is implicated only when a search is performed by the government.

2.   Police investigative activity that does not intrude on a suspect's reasonable expectation of privacy is also not regulated by the Fourth Amendment. The following are *not* searches:

a.   *Investigation of matters exposed to open view.* Anything that can be seen, heard, or smelled by members of the public from a vantage point where the officer is lawfully present is said to be in "open view." Officers may also use flashlights, binoculars, telescopes, cameras, and aerial surveillance to enhance their ability to make an observation from a lawful vantage point.

Bond v. United States—Part II.

b.   *Abandoned property.* A person who voluntarily abandons property relinquishes any privacy expectations in that property. This explains why contents of garbage cans placed on the curb for collection are not protected by the Fourth Amendment.

California v. Greenwood—Part II.

c.   *Canine examinations.* A sniff performed by a trained drug detection dog of luggage and other possessions does not constitute a search within the meaning of the Fourth Amendment because this procedure does not expose the contents to view and is incapable of revealing anything other than the presence of drugs, a contraband item in which suspects have no legitimate expectation of privacy. Canine examinations are discussed in greater depth in §§ 4.4, 5.7.

e.   *Duplication of private party searches.* Police duplication of a private party search is not considered a search if it goes no further than the search it follows, because duplication does not invade any reasonable expectations of privacy that have not already been invaded.

§ 4.3   —Sources of Search Authority

    A. For a search to be lawful, the officer must:

        1. *Act under a recognized source of search authority.* What is necessary to have search authority varies with the purpose of the search. The three main purposes of searching are: to discover evidence of a crime (called an evidentiary or full search), to disarm the suspect (called a limited weapons search), and to prepare a list of property the police have taken into custody (called an inventory search).

        2. *Confine the search activity to authorized search boundaries.* Each ground for search authority has companion rules delineating the boundaries of the search. Descriptions of search boundaries have two features: *scope* (i.e., the areas that may be searched) and *intensity* (i.e., the thoroughness with which these areas may be searched).

    B. *Full Searches.* Searches conducted to gather criminal evidence are called full searches. When the purpose of the search is to obtain evidence of crime, the Fourth Amendment *always*: (1) requires a search warrant or a recognized exception to the warrant requirement, and (2) limits the permissible scope and intensity of the search to activity directed toward finding the objects for which the officer has search authority. *Flippo v. West Virginia.* (Part II)

        1. *Searches under the Authority of a Warrant.*

            a. The Supreme Court has expressed a strong preference that searches for evidence be conducted under the authority of a search warrant.

            b. *Grounds for search authority.* To obtain a search warrant, the officer must demonstrate probable cause to believe that the specific objects linked to a crime will be found at a particular location. To demonstrate this, the officer must establish probable cause to believe that: (1) a crime has been committed, (2) specific objects linked to the crime exist, and (3) these objects are now located in the place to be searched.

            c. *Permissible search boundaries.* The warrant's description of the location to be searched defines the permissible scope of the search. Police may only search the location(s) described in the warrant. The warrant's description of the things to be seized defines the permissible intensity of the search. Police may only look in places in which the objects described in the warrant could fit.

2. Evidentiary searches conducted under an exception to the warrant requirement.

There are four exceptions to the warrant requirement that allow evidentiary searches: (I) consent, (ii) searches incident to a lawful custodial arrest, (iii) exigent circumstances, and (iv) searches of motor vehicles. These exceptions are discussed in greater depth later in this Chapter.

   a. Consent searches.

   Grounds for search authority. Only a person who has (or reasonably appears to have) joint access, control, and mutual use of the premises, vehicle, or other subject matter of the search may give a valid consent to search.

   Search boundaries. The scope of a consent search is limited to the area(s) police have been given consent to enter; the intensity of search activity is limited to looking for the expressed objects of the search. *Florida v. Jimeno*—Part II.

   b. Search incident to a lawful custodial arrest

   Grounds for search authority. A lawful custodial arrest carries with it the authority to conduct a search incident to the arrest. The purpose of recognizing this ground for search authority is to protect the arresting officer from weapon assaults and to prevent the arrestee from destroying evidence. A lawful custodial arrest is the only justification needed to conduct this search.

   Search boundaries. Because the purpose of a search incident to an arrest is to protect the arresting officer from a weapons assault and to prevent the arrestee from destroying evidence, search authority extends only to the arrestee's person and objects within the arrestee's immediate control (i.e., the area within grabbing distance). However, within these confines the search may be as intensive as necessary to discover weapons, contraband, or evidence of *any* crime. [Searches following a lawful custodial arrest are covered in §§4.8, 4.10 and 4.15 of this outline]. *United States v. Robinson* (Part II)

   c. Vehicle searches based on probable cause to believe that the vehicle contains criminal evidence or contraband.

   Grounds for search authority. Police may conduct a warrantless search of a vehicle whenever they have probable cause to believe that the vehicle contains contraband or evidence of criminal activity. The justification for this exception is the ease with which motor vehicles can be moved. The vehicle might be gone by the time the officer returns with a search warrant.

Search boundaries. Police may search any part of the vehicle—passenger compartment, glove compartment, or trunk—and any locked and unlocked containers in the vehicle that are capable of housing the object of their search. It does not matter who owns the containers; search authority extends to containers owned by the motorist, passengers, or third parties.

d.   Exigent circumstances

Grounds for search authority. Police are allowed to enter private premises without a search warrant when they are confronted with exigent circumstances that create an urgent need for immediate action. The three main circumstances that fall within this exception are hot pursuit of a fleeing suspect, threats to safety, and threatened destruction of evidence. [Exigent circumstances searches are covered in § 4.16]

Search boundaries. Exigent circumstances searches are limited, both in scope and intensity, to action immediately necessary to address the exigency that justified the entry. For example, if the entry is made is to prevent destruction of evidence, search activity is limited to searching the premises for persons who might destroy the evidence and securing the premises until a warrant can be obtained.

C.   *Limited weapons searches.* The purpose of a limited weapons search is to disarm a suspect so that an officer can conduct an investigation without fear for his or her safety. There are three kinds of limited weapons searches—frisks (covered in § 4.7), vehicular weapons searches (covered in §4.10), and protective sweeps (§ 4.15).

D.   *Inventory searches of impounded property.* After lawfully impounding a vehicle or an arrestee's clothing prior to jailing, police may perform an inventory search. The Fourth Amendment uses different criteria to assess the constitutionality of inventory searches. Inventory searches are covered in §§ 4.4, 4.8, and 4.12.

§4.4   —Seizures of Things under the Fourth Amendment

There are four reasons for seizing property: (1) to use it as evidence, (2) to detain it while conducting a brief investigation into its ownership or contents, (3) to prevent it from being moved while applying for a search warrant, and (4) to impound it. As with searches, Fourth Amendment requirements vary with the reason for the seizure.

A. Seizure defined

1. A seizure in the Fourth Amendment sense occurs when police commit *a meaningful interference* with a person's *possessory interest*. The key terms are "meaningful interference" and "possessory rights."

    a. *Meaningful interference.* To constitute a meaningful interference with possession, the police must assert dominion and control over property by removing it from the person's custody, detaining it, and refusing to allow the person to take it with him or her, or preventing the person from retrieving it from a third party.

        i. Touching or moving a traveler's luggage outside the traveler's presence is not a seizure if the acts of the police do not damage the luggage, delay its arrival, or interfere with the owner's travel plans

    b. *Possessory rights in property.* Exercise of dominion and control over abandoned property is not a seizure because a person who abandons property voluntarily relinquishes all property rights in it

B. *Seizure of property for use as evidence.* An officer may seize property for use as evidence only when the officer has: (1) probable cause to believe that it is connected to a crime, and (2) either a search warrant describing it or a plain view discovery.

1. *Probable cause to believe that the object furnishes evidence of a crime.* There are four categories officers may seize:

    a. fruits of a crime, which includes stolen goods and profits from criminal activity;

    b. instrumentalities of a crime, which include the tools and weapons used to perpetrate it;

    c. contraband, which includes any property the possession of which is illegal, such as unregistered guns and narcotics; and

    d. "other evidence," which includes any other object that is linked to a crime, such as a mask worn by a bank robber or a receipt for the purchase of the murder weapon.

2. *A search warrant listing the object or a plain view discovery.* Police must, in addition, have either a search warrant describing the object or discover the object in plain view within the confines of a lawful search.

a. *Seizure under a warrant listing the object.* A valid search warrant listing an object satisfies both requirements for lawful seizure because a determination has already been made by the magistrate that there is probable cause to believe that the objects described in the warrant are connected to a crime. All the officer has to do is locate them.

b. *Seizure of evidence in plain view.* The only time officers are allowed to seize criminal evidence or articles of contraband without a search warrant describing them is when they comes into plain view within the confines of a lawful search. For evidence to be considered in plain view:

   i. First, police must have a legitimate reason for being present at the precise location where the discovery is made or, as the first requirement is often stated, the initial intrusion that brought the officer in contact with the evidence must be lawful. The first requirement is satisfied if the police discover the object while they are executing a search warrant to search for other evidence, while they are conducting an appropriately limited search under any of the numerous exceptions to the warrant requirement, while they are inventorying the contents of an impounded vehicle, while they are rendering emergency aid to a motorist who is having a seizure, or while they are walking up a driveway to ring the doorbell to ask the occupant a few questions. The possibilities are unlimited.

   ii. The object's incriminating nature must be immediately apparent, which is another way of saying that the officer must acquire probable cause to believe that the object viewed is criminal evidence or contraband with no additional exploratory activity beyond that which is authorized; if further search activity is necessary to make this determination, the plain view doctrine does not apply.

   Arizona v. Hicks—Part II.

   United States v. Weinbender—Part II.

   iii. Finally, the officer must be able to gain physical access to the object to seize it without violating the Fourteenth Amendment. If a physical intrusion into a constitutionally protected location is necessary to gain access, the officer must obtain a search warrant or consent to enter.

C. *Brief, limited seizures.* Brief, limited seizures are generally used to detain closed containers like briefcases, suitcases, and mailed parcels, either to: (1) prevent them from being moved while the officer applies for a search warrant or (2) conduct a brief investigation.

1. Opening a closed container is *always* a search. Consequently, the officer must have a search warrant or be operating under an established exception to the warrant clause that allows containers to be opened.

2. Temporary seizures pending the issuance of a search warrant

Police may seize a container while applying for a search warrant to examine the contents: (1) when they have probable cause to believe that the container houses criminal evidence or contraband, and (2) there is a risk that the container may be moved or the contents destroyed during the time it takes to obtain a warrant.

3. Brief, limited seizures for investigation

   a. Based on the principles established in *Terry v. Ohio*, police have authority to seize an object in order to conduct a brief investigation when they reasonably suspect that the object or its contents is connected to a crime. However, they may not open a closed container without the owner's consent because this involves a search.

   b. Investigatory seizures are used most often in drug interdiction. When the police have a reasonable suspicion that a traveler's luggage contains narcotics, the police may seize it from the traveler's custody and detain it briefly to subject it to a canine examination. Because canine examinations are not regarded as searches [see §4.2 of this outline], the only requirement necessary to perform this procedure is grounds for a temporary seizure (i.e., a reasonable suspicion that the luggage contains drugs). *United States v. Place* (Part II, Chapter 3)

   c. Canine examinations may be performed without any degree of suspicion when police are in a position to perform it without a seizure. Canine examinations of checked luggage and cars stopped for a traffic violation require no degree of suspicion because there is no meaningful interference with the suspect's possessory rights in the property (i.e., no seizure).

D. *Seizures of vehicles and personal belongings for impoundment.*

   1. The Fourth Amendment does not require probable cause or a warrant to seize property for a noninvestigative reason, such as to impound it.

   2. Once property is impounded, a search will be conducted to produce an inventory. The Fourth Amendment regulates seizures for impoundments and inventory searches, but not by the same standards that are used to evaluate evidentiary searches and seizures.

3. For an impoundment and inventory search to be valid, (1) there must be a law or regulation authorizing impoundment, and (2) the inventory search must be conducted according to standardized operating procedures that establish clear guidelines for where, when, and how inventory searches are to be conducted. (Inventory searches are discussed further in §§4.8 and 4.12)

F. Review questions

1. Officer Blake, while executing a search warrant to search Sam's home for a stolen piano, saw a plastic bag of marijuana on top of a desk in the living room. She seized the bag and decided to look inside the desk drawers to see if there was more. She found three additional bags of marijuana in the top drawer and seized them also. Was the first bag of marijuana properly seized? Were the other three?

2. Sam was on a Greyhound bus that pulled into a rest stop. After all of the passengers had exited the bus to buy refreshments, stretch their legs, and do other things, Officer Green boarded the bus with Buff, a trained drug detection dog, and performed a drug sweep. The sweep consisted of removing all bags located in overhead compartments, placing them on the seat below, and having Buff sniff them. Buff alerted to a maroon bag. Green put all the bags back in the overhead compartments before the passengers returned to the bus and, after they reboarded, inquired whether any of them owned a maroon bag. When no one claimed the maroon bag, Officer Green removed it from the bus, opened it, and examined the contents. On discovering 24 grams of crack cocaine, along with a driver's license with Sam's picture on it, he reboarded the bus and arrested Sam. At his trial for possession of cocaine, Sam moved to suppress the evidence on the grounds that it was obtained through an illegal search and seizure. The purpose of this exercise is to determine whether Officer Green performed any act that the Fourth Amendment treats either as a search or a seizure. (1) Did Officer Green's removal of Sam's bag from the overhead compartment and putting it on the seat below constitute a *seizure* within the meaning of the Fourth Amendment? (2) Did exposing Sam's bag to an examination by Buff constitute a *search*? (3) Did Officer Green's removal of Sam's bag from the bus when no one claimed it constitute a *seizure*? (4) Did Officer Green's subsequent opening of Sam's bag and examining the contents constitute a *search*?

§4.5   —The Fourth Amendment Search Warrant

A. *Application for a search warrant.* Application for a search warrant is made by preparing a sworn affidavit. The affidavit requirements for a search warrant are identical to those for an arrest warrant in all respects except one. Probable cause for a search warrant requires probable cause to believe the evidence of a crime will be found at a particular location. To establish probable cause for the issuance of a search warrant, the officer's affidavit must set forth facts sufficient to justify a person of reasonable prudence in believing that: (1) a crime has been committed, (2) specific articles exist that furnish evidence of this crime, and (3) these articles are *now* located in the place to be searched.

B. *Form and content of the warrant.* The Fourth Amendment requires that a search warrant "particularly describe" the place(s) to be searched and the items to be seized. The purpose of this requirement is to prevent general searches. The particularity requirement operates to confine the search to locations in which and articles for which probable cause to search has been established.

1. *Particularized description of the place to be searched.* The search warrant must describe the place to be searched with sufficient particularity to allow an executing officer who is unfamiliar with the facts to locate and identify it with reasonable certainty.

2. *Particularized description of the things to be seized.* A particularized description of the things to be seized is required to avoid: (1) mistaken seizures, and (2) unnecessary rummaging. The description should be specific enough to serve both purposes.

C. *The facially valid warrant.* A warrant that appears on its face to contain a particularized description of the place to be searched and the objects to be seized is called "facially valid." Even if the warrant is later ruled invalid, evidence seized under a facially valid warrant will be admissible so long as the executing officer had a good faith, reasonable belief in the warrant's validity. (See §4.17)

D. *Execution of search warrants.* The requirements for executing search warrants are identical to those for executing arrest warrants, except that:

1. A search warrant must be executed without unreasonable delay because the facts that supported the magistrate's determination of probable cause to believe that the object of the search is located on the described premises can grow stale with the passage of time due to the risk of its being moved. Warrants cease to be valid once serious doubts exist about whether the objects described in the warrant are still at the place to be searched.

2. After completing the search, police must prepare an inventory of the property seized, give the owner a copy, and then return the warrant, together with a copy of the inventory, to the judge designated in the warrant.

The remaining sections in this chapter relate the concepts discussed above to the three general settings in which police are called upon to apply the rules: searches involving persons, searches involving vehicles, and searches involving premises. Examining the rules a second time in the settings in which police officers are called upon to apply them will solidify them and fix them in memory.

§4.6   Searches Involving Persons and Objects under their Immediate Control

Most searches involving persons and objects under their immediate control are performed without a warrant under the exceptions for weapon frisks, searches incident to arrest, or inventory searches incident to booking a person into jail.

§4.7   —The *Terry* Search Revisited

A. *Grounds for search authority.* A protective weapons search requires both: (1) a lawful stop based on reasonable suspicion of criminal activity and (2) a reasonable suspicion that the person with whom the officer is dealing is armed or could be dangerous. The crime under investigation, knowledge of the detainee's criminal past, weapon-like bulges in the detainee's clothing, hostile behavior, furtive gestures, and the late hour or secluded location of the stop are some of the factors that might justify a frisk.

B. *Search boundaries.* The purpose of a *Terry* weapons frisk is to protect the officer's safety so that the officer can pursue the investigation without fear of violence—*not* to discover evidence of crime.

1. *Scope.* A *Terry* frisk is limited to the suspect's person and containers within grabbing distance that the officer has reason to believe contain a weapon.

2. *Intensity.* The intensity of a *Terry* frisk is limited to patting down the suspect's outer clothing and making a cursory examination of the contents of containers. If the officer sees or feels what appears to be a weapon, he or she may reach into pockets, beneath clothing, etc. to seize it. All search activity must cease once the officer determines that the suspect is unarmed.

3. *Seizure of evidence in plain view during a Terry pat-down search.* Although police officers may not initiate a pat-down search solely because they suspect that a detainee has contraband on his or her person, they may seize it if they discover it in the course of a lawful pat-down. The plain view doctrine has an analogue known as the "plain feel" doctrine that applies to *Terry* searches. If an officer feels an object during a lawful pat-down search and its contours and mass make it immediately apparent that the object is contraband, the officer may seize it without a warrant. However, if additional touching, feeling, or manipulation is required to determine the

object's identity, *Terry* weapons frisk boundaries are exceeded and the plain touch doctrine does not apply.

4.   *State v. Wilson*—Part II

§4.8   —Search Following a Custodial Arrest

A.   *Grounds for search authority.* Authority to perform a search incident to arrest arises whenever an officer makes a lawful custodial arrest for *any* offense. Although the justification for this search authority is the need to disarm suspects and prevent them from destroying evidence, the officer need not have probable cause to believe that the arrestee has weapons or evidence of a crime in his possession. However, there must be an actual arrest; this ground for search authority does not arise if an officer, having probable cause for an arrest, decides instead to issue a citation.

1.   *United States v. Robinson*—Part II.

B.   *Search boundaries.* The justification for search authority incident to an arrest is the need to disarm the arrestee before taking him or her into custody and to prevent the arrestee from destroying evidence. The lawful objects of this search include contraband, evidence of *any* crime, and weapons. The scope of the officer's search authority extends to the arrestee's person, apparel, pockets, wallet, etc. and everything in the arrestee's possession or under his or her "immediate control" (defined as the area into which the arrestee might reach to retrieve a weapon or destroy evidence). Within these confines, the search may be as intense as necessary to discover even the "tiniest smidgen" of evidence.

1.   *Chimel v. California*—Part II.

C.   *Timing of searches incident to arrest.* Searches of the area under the suspect's immediate control and containers within arm's reach must be roughly contemporaneous with the arrest and an integral part of the arrest process. However, a special rule exists for searches involving the suspect's clothing, wallet, or handbag. Police may search them at the scene of the arrest, when the suspect arrives at the place of detention, or at both places.

D.   *Inventory searches incident to booking an arrestee into jail.* During routine booking procedures incident to incarceration, the suspect's clothing and other possessions will be impounded and an inventory search will be performed. The purpose of an inventory search is not to discover evidence. The purpose is to secure the arrestee's valuables, protect the police department against false claims of theft, and prevent weapons and contraband from being introduced into the jail community.

1.   *Grounds for search authority.* Because inventory searches serve a non-investigative purpose, probable cause and a search warrant

are unnecessary. However, inventory searches must be conducted according to routine police department inventory procedures. This is to prevent inventory searches from being misused for investigative purposes.

2. *Search boundaries.* Police may examine the arrestee's possessions as thoroughly, but only as thoroughly, as the department's inventory procedures allow. If evidence of a crime comes into plain view without exceeding the boundaries of the department's inventory procedures, police may seize it.

E. *Searches preceding an arrest.* A search conducted immediately before an arrest can qualify as a search incident to arrest only if grounds for making the arrest already exist and do not depend on the fruits of the search.

§4.9　　Searches Involving Vehicles

A. Most motor vehicle searches are conducted without a warrant. There are four theories for searching motor vehicles without a warrant in addition to consent: vehicular limited weapons searches, searches incident to the arrest of a motorist or passenger, searches based on probable cause to believe that the vehicle contains criminal evidence or contraband, and inventory searches of vehicles that have been impounded.

§4.10　　—Searches of Vehicles Pursuant to Detention or Arrest

A. *Terry* vehicle weapons search

1 *Grounds for search authority.* An officer who makes a lawful *Terry* or traffic stop may search the passenger compartment for weapons only if the officer has reasonable suspicion that weapons are located inside.

2. *Search boundaries.* Police are limited to searching for weapons. They may perform a cursory visual inspection of areas and containers inside the passenger compartment that are capable of housing a weapon.

B. Vehicle searches incident to the custodial arrest of an occupant

1. *Grounds for search authority.* Police must lawfully arrest either the driver or a passenger while they are still seated in the vehicle or after they have just exited; the arrest may be for *any* offense.

2. *Search boundaries.* The lawful objects of the search include weapons, contraband, and evidence of *any* crime. Police may search the entire passenger compartment (i.e., seats, floor, glove compartments, consoles, etc.) and everything inside the passenger compartment (i.e., luggage, handbags, boxes, bags, briefcases, clothing,

etc.), but not the engine area or trunk. The intensity may be as thorough as necessary to find even the "tiniest smidgen" of evidence.

3. *Timing of the search.* The search must be conducted shortly after the arrest and before either the arrestee or the vehicle has been moved from the scene.

§4.11   —Search of Vehicles on Probable Cause ("Automobile Exception")

A. *Grounds for search authority.* Police may search a motor vehicle without a warrant whenever they have probable cause to believe that contraband or criminal evidence is located inside a motor vehicle. This exception is based on the ease with which motor vehicles can be moved and the reduced expectation of privacy of motor vehicle occupants.

B. *Search boundaries.* Search authority extends to the entire vehicle from bumper to bumper. Police may search any part of the vehicle—passenger compartment, glove compartment, trunk, under seats, behind panels, etc.—in which the objects of their search might be found. They may also open packages and containers inside the vehicle large enough to house the objects of their search, regardless of their ownership and without holding them, pending issuance of a search warrant.

1. *Wyoming v. Houghton*—Part II.

C. *Timing of search.* Police may search the vehicle at the scene or wait until it reaches the impoundment lot. The timing of the search has virtually no bearing on validity.

§4.12   —Inventory Searches of Impounded Vehicles

A. *Grounds for search authority.* For an inventory search of an impounded motor vehicle to satisfy Fourth Amendment requirements: (1) police must have legal authority to impound the vehicle, (2) the decision to impound must be reasonable, and (3) the search must be conducted according to standardized procedures for inventorying the contents of impounded vehicles.

B. *Search Boundaries.* The scope and intensity of the search must conform to the department's inventory procedures. Search activity must be directed toward: (1) safeguarding valuables inside the vehicle; (2) protecting the police department against unjustified claims for loss or damage; or (3) locating potentially hazardous articles like weapons and flammables

§4.13   —Searches of Protected Premises

A. General searches of colonists' homes was the chief evil against which the Fourth Amendment was directed. Police may not enter a home or private business premises without a search warrant unless the entry is: (1) made with consent, or (2) justified by exigent circumstances.

B. Review Question 36 tests understanding of this material.

§4.14   —Premises Protected by the Fourth Amendment

A. *Home.* A "home," for purposes of the Fourth Amendment, means any place that serves as a residence, even if only for a short time. It includes houses, apartments, mobile homes, hotel and motel rooms, and homes in which the suspect resides as an overnight guest.

   1. *Curtilage.* Fourth Amendment protection for the home also extends to areas immediately surrounding the home, to which the ordinary activities of home life extend. This area is called the *curtilage.* Courts use the following criteria to decide whether a particular area is within the curtilage: its proximity to the dwelling, whether it is included within an area surrounding the dwelling that is enclosed by a fence, whether the area is used to support the normal activities of the home (such as a garage or a vegetable garden), and the steps taken by the residents to protect the area from public view.

      a. *United States v. Dunn*—Part II.

   2. *Open fields.* "Open fields" is a phrase used to describe undeveloped land that is not within the curtilage. The Supreme Court has determined that owners lack a reasonable expectation of privacy in "open fields." Accordingly, police do not need search authority to search outdoor spaces beyond the curtilage. While police may approach and look inside the windows of outbuildings, such as barns, that are located in open fields, they may not enter them without search authority.

B. *Business premises.* Fourth Amendment protection for business premises turns on whether they are open to the public. Police do not need a search warrant to go anyplace that members of the public are invited to enter. However, entry upon premises that are not open to the public, such as private offices and areas inside business establishments to which members of the public have no right of access constitutes a search.

§4.15   —Entry and Search of Premises Under a Warrant

A. *Boundaries of search authority conferred by a search warrant.* When a search warrant describes the place to be searched by address, search authority extends to the dwelling, all structures and grounds inside the curtilage, and also vehicles parked inside the curtilage. The permissible intensity of the search is controlled by the warrant's description of the items to be seized; police may search any place or container on the premises in which any of the objects described in the warrant could fit, regardless of ownership.

1. *Authority to detain the occupants during execution of a search warrant.* The issuance of a search warrant automatically carries authority to detain persons who regularly occupy the premises during the execution of the warrant. Authority to detain persons who are not regular occupants requires particularized reasonable suspicion that they are connected to the crime underlying the search warrant.

    a.   *Muehler v. Mena*—Part II.

2. *Authority to frisk the occupants for weapons.* Issuance of a search warrant does not carry automatic authority to frisk the occupants for weapons. A weapons frisk requires a reasonable suspicion that the person frisked is armed or could be dangerous.

3. *Authority to search the occupants for objects* listed in the warrant. A search warrant authorizes the search of things, not people. Police may not search persons found on the premises for objects listed in the search warrant unless: (1) the search warrant expressly grants this authority by naming the person or a class to which the person belongs, (2) the search is conducted as an incident to a lawful arrest, or (3) there is probable cause to believe that the person searched has objects described in the warrant on their person.

C. *Search authority conferred by an arrest warrant.* When police arrest a person under a search warrant inside the person's home, they may:

1. Search the premises to the degree necessary to locate the suspect.

2. After making the arrest, police have automatic authority to perform a "protective sweep." A protective sweep is limited to a cursory visual inspection of closets and other spaces *immediately adjoining* the place of arrest in which would-be attackers could hide. Police must have reasonable suspicion that persons who pose a danger to them are actually present on the premises to perform a larger sweep.

3. Perform a search incident to arrest in accordance with the rules outlined in § 4.8 above.

§4.16   Entry and Search of Premises under a Warrant Exception

There are only two bases for searching private premises without a search warrant: (1) exigent circumstances, and (2) consent.

A. Exigent circumstances

1. *Grounds for search authority.* The exigent circumstances exception authorizes the police to make a warrantless entry when:

a. they have reason to believe that life or property is in imminent danger or that a serious crime is in progress;

    i. *Brigham City, Utah v. Stuart*—Part II.

b. they have probable cause to believe that incriminating evidence or contraband is located on the premises and an objectively reasonable belief that the evidence will be destroyed or removed unless they act immediately; or

c. they are in hot pursuit of a suspect whom they have probable cause to arrest for a serious crime who flees and takes refuge inside.

2. *Search boundaries.* When an entry is made under the exigent circumstances exception, search authority is limited to actions immediately necessary to address the exigency that justified the entry. For example, when entry is made to prevent destruction of evidence, the police may perform a cursory visual inspection of rooms, closets, and other locations in which persons who might destroy the evidence could hide. If the evidence sought is discovered in plain view while the police are performing a cursory visual inspection, the police may seize it under the plain view doctrine. If no evidence is discovered, the police must secure the premises and then apply for a search warrant.

3. *Review question.* While patrolling a residential neighborhood late at night, Officer Collins heard the sound of breaking glass followed by a burglar alarm. Concerned that a burglary was in progress, Collins entered the house through the unlocked front door and began searching for the suspected intruder. While looking under a bed in the front bedroom, he found a bag of marijuana and seized it. When he reached the kitchen, he discovered why the alarm had gone off. A fallen tree branch had broken the kitchen window, causing a motion detector to set it off. The owner of the house has moved to suppress the bag of marijuana. What should the result be?

B. *Consent.* A valid consent will justify a warrantless entry onto private premises.

1. *Actual consent.* Actual consent given by a person who appears to have authority is necessary in order to enter a home or its curtilage. The requirements for a valid consent search were previously covered in §4.3 of this outline.

2. *Implied consent to administrative searches.* Statutes often grant government agencies charged with enforcement of government regulations the authority to conduct warrantless inspections of businesses to check for compliance. Courts have upheld such authority on the theory that a person who undertakes a business impliedly consents to inspections required by law.

§4.17   The Exclusionary Rule

A.   *Statement of the exclusionary rule.* The exclusionary rule is a judicially created remedy developed by the Supreme Court to deter police violations of the Fourth Amendment. It requires suppression of evidence derived directly or indirectly from an illegal search. The exclusionary rule applies both in state and federal courts.

    1.   *Mapp v. Ohio*—Part II

B.   *Standing.* Only a person whose Fourth Amendment rights were violated by an illegal search and seizure may challenge introduction of illegally obtained evidence. This is known as "standing." If the police illegally search A's home and find evidence that incriminates B, B lacks standing to object to introduction of this evidence against him because his privacy was not invaded.

C.   *Exceptions to the exclusionary rule.* The Supreme Court has recognized the following exceptions to the exclusionary rule.

    1.   *Inevitable discovery.* Suppression of evidence obtained through an illegal search and seizure is not required if the court finds that the evidence would have been discovered through lawful means had the illegal search not occurred.

    2.   *Good faith.* Suppression is not required of evidence obtained in violation of the Fourth Amendment if the court finds that the officer who performed the search acted in objective good faith. The most common application of the good faith exception is good faith reliance on a facially valid search warrant that is later determined to be defective. This exception is designed to encourage officers to apply for search warrants by permitting evidence seized under a defective warrant to be used when the executing officers have a good faith belief in the warrant's validity, and their belief is objectively reasonable.

    3.   *Illegality in the Manner of Entering to Execute a Valid Search Warrant.* Suppression is regarded as too drastic a remedy when the illegality relates solely to the method of entry under an otherwise valid search warrant.

        a.   *Hudson v. Michigan*—Part II.

    4.   *Impeachment.* Although illegally seized evidence may not be offered by the prosecution to prove the defendant's guilt, it may be used to impeach (i.e., discredit) the defendant's own testimony if the defendant takes the stand and gives false testimony.

5. *Use outside the criminal context.* Although the exclusionary rule bars introduction of illegally seized evidence to establish a defendant's guilt at his or her criminal trial, there are a number of proceedings—such as grand jury hearings, parole hearings, and civil trials—to which the exclusionary does not apply and in which illegally seized evidence can be admitted.

Review Questions

1. What was the historical abuse that led to the adoption of the search and seizure clause of the Fourth Amendment? (§4.2)

2. How did the Supreme Court define the term "search" prior to *Katz v. United States*? (§4.2)

3. How is the term "search" defined today? (§4.2)

4. A search (i.e., intrusion on a reasonable expectation of privacy) can occur in one of two ways. What are the two ways? (§4.2)

5. What four locations are mentioned in the Fourth Amendment as having constitutional protection? (§4.2)

6. An irate employee breaks into his boss's locked file cabinet, steals an incriminating letter that bears his employer's signature, and takes it to the police. Has there been a search within the meaning of the Fourth Amendment? May the police use the stolen letter as evidence? (§4.2)

7. When is something considered in "open view?" Why are police observations of matters in open view not considered searches? (§4.2)

8. Do any of the following police investigative activities involve searches within the meaning of the Fourth Amendment? Explain why or why not. (§4.2)
   a. Looking inside the passenger compartment of a car, parked on a public street, without opening the door.
   b. Shining a flashlight to illuminate the interior of the automobile so the officer can see better.
   c. Getting on the ground, looking underneath the automobile, and inspecting the tires.
   d. Walking a drug detection dog around an automobile to sniff for illegal drugs.
   e. Opening the automobile door and looking inside the glove compartment.
   f. Squeezing soft luggage to determine the contents.

9. Searches for criminal evidence are called "full searches." What does the Fourth Amendment require for a full search? (§4.3)

10. There are four exceptions to the warrant requirement that permit full searches. Identify them. (§4.3)

11. What is the purpose of a limited weapons search? When does the Fourth Amendment require for police officers to perform a limited weapons search? (§4.3)

12. What is the purpose of an inventory search? On what occasions are inventory searches likely to be conducted? What does the Fourth Amendment require for an inventory search? (§4.3)

13. Define the term *seizure*. (§4.4)

14. Indicate whether the following police actions involve a seizure and explain why or why not. (§4.4)
    a. Taking things out of a garbage can put on the curb for collection and keeping them.
    b. Removing checked luggage from an airport baggage cart, subjecting it to a canine examination, and putting it back in time for the luggage to be placed on the intended flight.

15. What does the Fourth Amendment require to seize property for use as evidence? (§4.4)

16. Identify the four categories of articles that may be seized as evidence. (§4.3)

17. What three conditions are necessary to seize criminal evidence under the plain view doctrine? (§4.4)

18. Suppose police, while executing a search warrant to search for drugs, find a spiral notebook, open it, and read the contents. The notebook contains records of recent sales. May the police seize it under the plain view exception? (§4.4)

19. Suppose the police, while investigating a domestic complaint in the neighboring home, observe marijuana plants growing in Sam's fenced backyard. May they enter through the gate and seize the plants under the plain view doctrine? (§ 4.4)

20. Under what circumstances may an officer temporarily detain a container pending the issuance of a search warrant? (§ 4.4)

21. Under what circumstances may an officer subject a container to a canine examination? (§4.4)

22. What four things does the language of the Fourth Amendment require for the issuance of a search warrant? (§4.5)

23. What three things must an officer's affidavit establish to support a finding of *probable cause* for the issuance of a search warrant? (§4.5)

24. Why does the Fourth Amendment require that search warrants contain a particularized description of the place to be searched and the things to be seized? (§4.5)

25. What is necessary for a search warrant to be considered facially valid?

26. What are the advantages of conducting a search under a warrant, as opposed to acting under a warrant clause exception?

27. How do the requirements governing the execution of a search warrant differ from those governing the execution of an arrest warrant? (§4.5)

28. What is necessary for a police officer to have authority to conduct a *Terry* weapons frisk? What is the permissible scope of this search? What is the permissible intensity? When, if ever, may police seize items other than weapons discovered during a limited weapons search? (§4.7)

29. What is the justification for the search incident to an arrest exception? What is the permissible scope of the search? What does the phrase "under the arrestee's control" mean? What is the permissible intensity? What is the permissible time frame for conducting a search incident to an arrest? What kinds of items may be seized during a search incident to an arrest? (§4.8)

30. When may an officer open a closed container as part of the search authority that arises incident to an arrest? (§4.8)

31. Which of the various exceptions to the search warrant requirement studied in this chapter applies to motor vehicles? (§4.9)

32. When do police have the authority to conduct a vehicular limited weapons search? What parts of the vehicle may be searched? What is the permissible intensity of the search? (§4.10)

33. What parts of the vehicle may be searched incident to the arrest of the driver? What is the permissible intensity of this search? (§4.10)

34. What justifications has the Supreme Court advanced for recognizing an exception to the warrant requirement when police have probable cause to believe that a motor vehicle contains evidence subject to seizure? What parts of the vehicle may be searched under this exception? What is the permissible intensity of searches conducted under this exception? When must the search be performed? (§4.11)

35. What is necessary to perform an inventory search of an impounded vehicle? What are the permissible scope and intensity of this search? (§4.12)

36. When, if ever, may the police physically enter a residence without a warrant of any kind? (§§4.13-4.16)

37. Define the terms curtilage and *open fields*. (§4.14)

38. When does an officer need Fourth Amendment search authority to enter business premises? (§4.14)

39. Describe the scope of the search authority conferred by a search warrant that describes the location to be searched by address. (§4.15)

40. When may police detain persons on the premises covered by a search warrant? (§4.15)

41. When may police frisk persons on the premises covered by a search warrant? (§4.15)

42. When may police search persons on the premises covered by a search warrant for objects listed in the warrant? (§4.15)

43. What is the purpose of a protective sweep? What are the normal boundaries of a protective sweep? When may police extend the boundaries of a protective sweep? What is the intensity of a protective sweep? (§4.15)

44. What three circumstances are considered sufficiently exigent to justify a warrantless entry onto private premises? What is necessary to have authority to enter under each circumstance? What search activity is permissible when a warrantless entry is made to prevent destruction of evidence? (§4.16)

45. Who has standing to challenge the introduction of illegally seized evidence? (§4.17)

46. What are the five exceptions to the exclusionary rule? (§4.17)

47. What two conditions are necessary for illegally seized evidence to be admissible under the good faith exception to the exclusionary rule? (§4.17)

Chapter 5
Laws Governing
Police Surveillance

Objectives

Chapter 5 covers Fourth Amendment and federal statutory regulation of police surveillance. The student should leave this chapter with an understanding of:

1. Fourth Amendment restrictions on conventional surveillance.

2. Fourth Amendment restrictions on the use of police surveillance technologies, such as electronic tracking devices, video surveillance cameras, narcotics detection dogs, metal detectors, thermal imagers, pen/trap devices, etc.

3. The federal Wiretap Act's statutory scheme for regulating interception of protected communications with a device, namely: (1) the definition of an interception; (2) prohibition of interception without prior court approval; (3) steps necessary to obtain court approval; (4) legal controls surrounding the execution of interception orders; and (5) restrictions on disclosure of intercepted communications.

4. Communications surveillance that is not regulated by the Wiretap Act, namely: (1) listening with the unaided ear, (2) interceptions of oral communication where the target lacks a reasonable expectation of freedom from interception, and (3) interceptions conducted by or with the consent of a party.

5. Statutory protection for e-mail, voice mail, and text messages under the federal Wiretap Act and the Stored Wire and Electronic Communications and Transactional Records Act and when each statute applies.

6. The Foreign Intelligence Surveillance Act's scheme for regulating the use of electronic surveillance to collect foreign intelligence.

Discussion Outline

§5.1   Introduction to the Laws Governing Police Surveillance

In modern times, it is not unusual for police to use a host of surveillance techniques in a single investigation, such as wiretapping, interception of e-mail messages, video surveillance, and use of electronic tracking devices. This chapter discusses the constitutional and statutory rules that apply to police surveillance. It builds on the search and seizure principles developed in Chapter 4.

§5.2   Fourth Amendment Foundation of Police Surveillance Law: The *Katz* Standard

A. *Historical development.* The Supreme Court's first bout with privacy-invasive police surveillance technology involved wiretapping. In *Olmstead v. United States*, decided in 1928, the Supreme Court ruled that wiretapping was not a "search" or a "seizure" under the Fourth Amendment because a search required a physical intrusion into a constitutionally protected location and a "seizure" required the taking of something tangible.

1. *Olmstead v. United States*—Part II.

B. The *Katz* standard. Forty years later, in *Katz v. United States*, the Supreme Court discarded the *Olmstead* definition of a search and adopted the contemporary definition. A search occurs when police intrude on a suspect's *reasonable expectation of privacy*, whether the intrusion is physical or technological.

1. *Katz v. United States*—Part II.

2. Shortly after *Katz*, Congress enacted the federal Wiretap Act, which requires law enforcement officials to obtain a wiretap order (i.e., a specialized search warrant) to engage in wiretapping and electronic surveillance.

§5.3   Application of the *Katz* Standard to Conventional Surveillance

Most of the rules that govern technologically assisted surveillance evolved from principles developed earlier in cases involving conventional surveillance. The three principles described below are of central importance in police surveillance law and continuously reemerge in slightly changed forms throughout the entire field.

A. *Police surveillance of matters exposed to public view is not a search.* Police are free to investigate using their natural senses in any location where they are lawfully present because suspects have no reasonable expectation of privacy in illegal activities conducted in a place where they can be seen, heard, or otherwise detected by members of the public.

B. *The homes carry heightened protection under the Fourth Amendment.*

1. The home is a privacy zone that police are not allowed to enter without a search warrant. Protection for the home extends to the *curtilage*. Surveillance of the suspect's home may not be conducted from a vantage point inside the curtilage without a search warrant.

2. The area that lies beyond the boundary of the curtilage is called an "*open field*." Police do not need any Fourth Amendment justification to enter an open field, although their presence constitutes a trespass under property law. In *United States v. Dunn* (Part II, Chapter 3), the Supreme Court stated that "there is no constitutional difference between police observations conducted while in a public place and while standing in an open field." Consequently, when police conduct their surveillance while standing in an open field, the suspect has no Fourth Amendment grounds for complaint, even if the matter surveilled is the interior of the suspect's home.

C. *Information voluntarily disclosed to a third party carries no Fourth Amendment protection.*

1. *Conversations between the suspect and a police informant.* Nothing a suspect voluntarily reveals to a police undercover agent or informant is protected by the Fourth Amendment. This principle was established in *Hoffa v. United States*, where the Supreme Court ruled that the Fourth Amendment does not protect a wrongdoer's misplaced belief that the person to whom he confides his wrongdoing will not pass the information on to the authorities. Once information has been voluntarily revealed, the suspect lacks any further constitutionally protected privacy interest in that information.

2. *Information contained in records and files in the hands of a third party.* The same principle applies to records and files in the hands of a third party. Nothing a suspect voluntarily reveals to a third party—bank records, charge card records, employment records, financial records, telephone and Internet service provider records, insurance records, car rental records, electricity bills, etc.—is protected by the Fourth Amendment.

§5.4 Application of the *Katz* Standard to Technologically Assisted Surveillance: An Overview

Fourth Amendment restrictions on use of police surveillance devices depends on the *nature of information obtained—whether it is in open view or hidden—not the type of device used to obtain it.*

A. *Technologically assisted surveillance of matters exposed to public view.* The Fourth Amendment does not restrict use of surveillance devices that enable police to observe more efficiently, cost-effectively, or at a greater distance matters in *open view*. Police are free to use flashlights, tele-scopes, tracking devices, video surveillance cameras, helicopters, etc. to enhance their ability to observe matters in the open view of the public.

B. *Technologically assisted surveillance of matters hidden from public view.* Use of surveillance technologies to monitor activities hidden from public view that a suspect reasonable expects are private results in a search and requires a search warrant.

   1. Because of the heightened protection for the home, police are not allowed to employ sensory-enhancing technologies, not in general public use, to acquire information about activities inside the home that are not visible from outside unless they have a search warrant.

   2. Wiretapping, bugging, and interception of electronic transmissions are now regulated by the Wiretap Act, which is covered in §§5.8-5.15 of this outline.

C. *Technologically assisted surveillance with the consent of a cooperating informant.* Because information voluntarily disclosed to a third party carries no Fourth Amendment protection, the Fourth Amendment does not restrict the secret use of audio or video surveillance equipment to monitor contacts between the suspect and a cooperating informant.

§5.5   —Electronic Tracking

A. *Beeper tracking of public movements.* Attachment of an electronic beeper to the undercarriage of a suspect's vehicle to monitor his public movements does not violate the Fourth Amendment because this activity is carried on in the open view of the public. However, the beeper must be installed while the suspect's vehicle is parked outside the curtilage; otherwise, the installation will violate the Fourth Amendment.

B. GPS tracking.

   The Supreme Court has not yet decided whether GPS surveillance con-stitutes a search under the Fourth Amendment. Lower federal courts generally hold that use of GPS tracking devices are governed by the same rules that apply to beepers.

C. Electronic Tracking of Objects Inside Homes and Other Protected Premises.

   Electronic beepers are sometimes attached to objects other than vehi-cles. Once a beeper-attached article is withdrawn from public view and taken inside a particular residence, continued monitoring of the beeper requires a search warrant.

D. *Use of the suspect's cell phone as a personal locator.*

§5.6   —Video Surveillance

A. Video surveillance of activities in open view.

   1. Police do not need a search warrant to use video cameras to moni-
       tor activities in full public view. Surveillance cameras may be used
       without a warrant in any location where an officer could lawfully
       make the observation in person.

   2. *United States v. McIver*—Part II.

B. Video surveillance of activities inside private homes and offices.

   1. A search warrant is necessary to install and use video surveillance
       equipment inside private homes, offices, and other locations pro-
       tected by the Fourth Amendment.

   2. A conventional search warrant is insufficient to authorize video
       surveillance. Because of the hyper-intrusive nature of secretly
       watching a person's activities inside his or her own home or office,
       courts have looked to the heightened procedural requirements con-
       tained in the Wiretap Act for guidance in framing video surveil-
       lance search warrants.

C. Video surveillance of interactions between the target and a cooperating
    informant.

   1. Police do not need a search warrant to conduct secret video surveil-
       lance of contacts between a suspect and a cooperating informant.
       Because the informant could have reported everything said and
       done in his presence from memory, secret video surveillance of the
       target's words and actions in the informant's presence does not vio-
       late the Fourth Amendment. However, the video surveillance must
       cease once the informant leaves.

   2. *United States v. Lee*—Part II.

D. Video surveillance that produces a soundtrack.

   1. If the government uses video equipment that produces a soundtrack,
       the video portion must satisfy the Fourth Amendment, while the
       audio portion must satisfy the Wiretap Act.

   2. Unless the suspect lacks a reasonable expectation of freedom from
       monitoring as, for example, where the equipment is installed and
       used in the visitors' room of a jail or a party to the taped conversa-
       tion consents, as in the International Boxing Foundation bribery
       case, a wiretap order will be necessary to use video equipment that
       produces a soundtrack.

D. Mass surveillance as a tool of social control.

§5.7   —Detection Devices

Detection devices disclose things that are incapable of being detected by the ordinary senses. This section explores Fourth Amendment restrictions on four widely used police detection devices—drug- and bomb-sniffing dogs, magnetometers, X-rays, and thermal detectors.

A.   Canine examination consent.

     1.   The Supreme Court regards use of trained narcotics detection dogs as "*sui generis*" because they disclose only the presence of narcotics, a contraband item, without providing information about lawful activity. Detection devices that detect only the presence of contraband—objects that it is always a crime to possess—are not regulated by the Fourth Amendment. Sadly, drug-sniffing dogs and chemical tests are the only devices currently available that react only to the presence of contraband.

     2.   Dog sniffs may be performed, with no suspicion at all, in any location where the officer is lawfully present on any object to which an officer has a lawful right of access. Otherwise, police need Fourth Amendment grounds to seize the object before they may expose it to a sniff.

B.   X-ray and magnetometer searches

     1.   Use of X-ray devices and magnetometers in airports, courthouses, jails, and other places with special security needs does not violate the Fourth Amendment. Although their use constitutes a search, the search is valid without a warrant under the administrative search exception to the warrant requirement. Searches conducted as part of a general regulatory scheme in furtherance of an administrative purpose (here preventing hijackings, bombings, and terrorist attacks using planes), rather than as part of a criminal investigation to secure evidence of a crime, are permissible under the Fourth Amendment without individualized suspicion when the government's need to conduct the search exceeds the invasion of privacy that the search entails.

     2.   *United State v. Hartwell*—Part II.

C.   Heat Sensors (Thermal-Imaging Devices)

     1.   Indoor marijuana gardens require heat lamps that produce substantial amounts of heat. Thermal imagers (heat sensors) create a picture based on heat emissions. When directed at a building suspected of being used to grow marijuana, the device can confirm those suspicions by detecting an abnormal heating pattern suggestive of a marijuana growing operation.

    2.   A search results whenever the police use sense-enhancing technologies that are not in general public use to obtain information about activities inside the home that are not visible from outside.

    3.   *Kyllo v. United State*—Part II.

§5.8   The Wiretap Act

    A.   Since 1968, interception of communications has been regulated by a federal statute known as the Wiretap Act. Enactment of the statute was made necessary by the Supreme Court's holding in *Katz v. United States* that a search warrant is required to secretly monitor telephone conversations.

§5.9   —Scope of the Wiretap

    A.   Meaning of interception. An "interception" is necessary to trigger application of the Wiretap Act. An "interception" occurs when: (1) *a device is used* (2) *to acquire access to the contents* (3) *of a protected communication during the course of its transmission.* These requirements are discussed in reverse order for clarity of presentation.

        1.   *Protected communication.* The Wiretap Act protects three kinds of communications:

           a.   Wire (i.e., communications containing the human voice that travel through wires at some point in their transmission);

           b.   Oral (i.e., communications carried by sound waves). Oral communications are protected only when they are "uttered by a person exhibiting an expectation that such communication is not subject to interception under circumstances justifying such expectation;" and

           c.   Electronic (i.e., signs, signals, writings, images, and other data transmitted over a wide range of mediums).

        2.   *To acquire access the contents.*

           a.   For an interception to occur, the device used must provide access to the *contents* of a protected communication. Devices that provide access to other information, such as the telephone numbers dialed to or from a particular phone, are beyond the scope of the Wiretap Act.

           b.   Furthermore, the access must be acquired while the message is being transmitted. The Wiretap Act protects e-mail, voice mail, and text messages only for the few fleeting seconds during which they are being transmitted. After this, they become stored communications. Access to stored wire and electronic communications is regulated by a separate federal statute, the Stored Wire and Electronic Communications and Transactional Records Act, which is covered in § 5.15 of this outline. Stored communications receive considerably less legal protection.

3. *Use of a device.* The Wiretap Act regulates use of *any* device, mechanical, electronic, or otherwise, that facilitates access to the contents of a protected communication in the course of transmission. The type of device does not matter.

§5.10   –Procedural Requirements for Intercepting Protected Communications

The procedural requirements for obtaining and executing a wiretap order exceed Fourth Amendment requirements for a conventional search warrant. The Wiretap Act:

A.   Limits the crimes for which wiretap orders may be issued to serious crimes.

B.   Requires approval by a high-ranking official within the Justice Department before the application may be submitted to the court.

C.   Requires proof that traditional investigative techniques have been tried and failed, appear unlikely to succeed, or are too dangerous to try.

D.   Requires establishment of probable cause to believe that: (1) a person is committing a crime for which an interception order may be issued; (2) the targeted facilities are being used in connection with that crime; and (3) an interception will produce communications relevant to that crime.

E.   Limits the duration of wiretap orders to a maximum of 30 days or attainment of the authorized objective, whichever occurs first. A fresh application is required for an extension.

F.   Requires that wiretap orders be executed so as to minimize intrusions into communications not related to the investigation.

G   Limits disclosure and use of communications intercepted under a wiretap order to: (1) furtherance of the investigation, (2) national defense and security, and (3) giving testimony in court.

§5.11   Communication Surveillance Not Regulated by the Wiretap Act

A wiretap order is not required to listen to the conversations of others when: (1) the conversation is overheard naturally (i.e., without the aid of a device), (2) the target of the surveillance lacks a justifiable expectation of freedom from interception, or (3) the interception is conducted by or with the consent of a party. These situations are explored in the next three sections.

§ 5.12   —Listening with the Unaided Ear

A. When government agents listen with their unaided ear, the only require-
    ments are those imposed by the Fourth Amendment. If the listening occurs
    in a place where the officer is lawfully present, no search results because
    people who speak loudly enough to be overheard by others in close prox-
    imity have knowingly exposed their conversation to the public.

B. Any conversation that is heard naturally may be secretly recorded with-
    out triggering application of the Wiretap Act because the tape recorder
    is not the means of "acquiring" the conversation; it is simply a means of
    preserving it.

C. Resort to technological devices is necessary to acquire a conversation
    when it is not otherwise accessible. When an oral conversation is obtained
    through artificial means, there is a chance that the Wiretap Act has been
    violated. Whether it has depends on whether the suspect had a reasonable
    expectation that the oral conversation would not be intercepted.

§ 5.13   —Interception of Communications Where the Target Lacks a Reasonable
          Expectation of Freedom From Interception

A. The Wiretap Act only protects oral communications when they are
    "uttered by a person exhibiting an expectation that such communica-
    tion is not subject to interception under circumstances justifying such
    expectation." Whether a person has a reasonable expectation of freedom
    from interception depends on a number of factors, the most important
    of which are the nature of the location, the presence and proximity of
    others, and how loudly the person speaks.

    1. *United States v. McIntyre*—Part II.

B. No reasonable expectation of freedom from interception is recognized
    in oral conversations carried on while third parties are close enough to
    be within normal hearing range. As a result, the conversation can be
    electronically intercepted without a wiretap order (bugged funeral urn
    case).

C. No reasonable expectation of freedom from interception exits in oral
    conversations carried on in highly controlled police environments like
    police stations, jails, prisons, and the backseats of patrol cars because
    monitoring is so common that it's almost expected. Such conversations
    can also be intercepted without a wiretap order.

    1. *United States v. Turner*—Part II.

§ 5.14   —Interception with the Consent of a Party

A. A wiretap order is not required to intercept wire, oral, or electronic commu-
    nications when the interceptor is a party to the communication or one of the
    parties to the communication has given prior consent to the interception.

B. Consent may be implied, as well as expressed. Consent will be implied when a person places a telephone call with notice that the call will be monitored. Implied consent is regularly used to justify the warrantless monitoring of prisoner phone calls.

    1. *United States v. Willoughby*—Part II.

§5.15   –Access to -Email, Voice Mail, and Text Messages

A. The Wiretap Act protects email, voice mail, and text message during the brief period of transmission. A wiretap order is necessary to intercept them while they are being transmitted.

B. Once they reach their destination, strong legal protection under the Wiretap Act ends. They become stored communications and access is controlled by the Stored Wire and Electronic Communications and Transactional Records.

    1. *United States v. Jones*—Part II.

C. Protection for stored communications is much weaker. For communications that have been in storage for more than 180 days, for example, access can often be obtain without notice to the subscriber on a showing as meager as an affidavit reciting that the information is likely to be relevant to a criminal investigation.

§ 5.16   –Pen Registers and Trap-and-Trace Devices

A. Pen registers and trap-and-traces are recording devices attached to a telephone line, usually at a central telephone office, that identify the source and destination of all calls made to (pen registers) or from (trap-and-trace devices) a particular telephone. Their use is not regulated by the Wiretap Act because they do not yield access to the *contents* of the call and, thus, there is no interception.

B. The Electronic Communications Privacy Act makes it illegal to install pen/ traps without a court order. Orders are readily obtainable. The only thing necessary is an application made under oath stating that the information likely to be obtained is relevant to an ongoing criminal investigation.

§ 5.17   Foreign Intelligence Surveillance Act

The Foreign Intelligence Surveillance Act (FISA) regulates domestic surveillance conducted for national security purposes.

A. FISA electronic surveillance authority may be sought only when the target of the surveillance is a foreign power or an agent of a foreign power, terms that include international terrorist organizations and their members.

B. Applications for FISA surveillance orders must be approved by the Attorney General, state the facts warranting a belief that the target of the surveillance is a foreign power or agent of a foreign power, describe the manner in which the order will be implemented, and contain the certification of a senior national security official that the information sought is foreign intelligence information and that the information cannot be obtained by normal investigative techniques.

C. Judicial oversight is minimal. The judge is required to approve the application if the information provided establishes probable cause to believe that the target is a foreign power or agent of a foreign power and the necessary certifications are attached.

Review Questions

1. In *Olmstead v. United States*, the Supreme Court ruled that wiretapping did not violate the Fourth Amendment. How did the Court define the term search? *Seizure*? (§5.2)

2. What impact did *Katz v. United States* have on *Olmstead*? How did the *Katz* court define the term *search*? (§5.2)

3. Congress responded to the *Katz* decision by enacting the Wiretap Act. What did the Supreme Court say in *Katz* that made enactment necessary? (§§ 5.2, 5.8)

4. Three principles of central importance in police surveillance law were introduced in §5.3. What were they? (§5.3)

5. A police officer crawls over Mary Wanna's fence and listens under her window as she conducts a series of drug transactions. Mary speaks in a tone loud enough to be heard only by someone standing under her window. Does this violate the Fourth Amendment? Which of the three principles discussed in §5.3 applies? (§5.3)

6. Police officers rent a motel room adjoining Mary Wanna's room and conduct surveillance of her conversations by pressing their ears against the common wall. The walls are thin and they are able to hear everything Mary says. Does this violate the Fourth Amendment? Which of the three principles discussed in §5.3 applies? (§5.3)

7. Police officers rent a motel room adjoining Mary Wanna's room to conduct surveillance of her conversations, but this time the walls are too thick for them to hear. They pay a motel cleaning lady to go into her room, listen as she cleans, and report everything she hears. She reports a highly incriminating conversation she overheard. Does this violate the Fourth Amendment? Which of the three principles discussed in §5.3 applies? (§5.3)

8. The overview of technologically assisted surveillance developed in §5.4 builds on the three principles that were introduced in §5.3. Make sure you recognize and understand the parallelism. (§5.4)

9. A new police surveillance device has recently come on the market. Super-Spy X-Ray Binoculars are a surveillance device that enables police to look through walls from a distance of up to 100 yards. While standing on a public street police look through Mary Wanna's walls and observe marijuana plants growing inside. Does this violate the Fourth Amendment? Which of the principles introduced in §5.3 and elaborated upon in §5.4 applies? (§5.4)

10. Suppose police, while standing on a public street, use ordinary binoculars to look through an open window in Mary Wanna's house and see the very same thing. Does this violate the Fourth Amendment? Which of the principles introduced in §5.3 and elaborated upon in §5.4 applies? What if the officer was standing on Mary's property in an open field outside the curtilage when he used binoculars to view the interior of her home. Would this change anything? (§5.4)

11. Suppose Judy Judas agrees to wear a concealed radio transmitter when she makes her next drug purchase from Mary Wanna. Mary speaks freely, unaware that Judy is wired for sound and that the police are listening. Does this violate the Fourth Amendment? Which of the principles introduced in §5.3 and elaborated upon in §5.4 applies? (§5.4)

12. When is electronic beeper surveillance *not* regulated by the Fourth Amendment? When is it regulated? Why has the line been drawn where it has? (§5.5)

13. When is video surveillance *not* regulated by the Fourth Amendment? When is it regulated? When is a wiretap order required for video surveillance? (§5.6)

14. The Whosville Police Department received a report from a highly reliable informant that Mary Wanna is a drug dealer who traffics in narcotics out of her home located at 1420 Fifth Avenue. Police would like to conduct electronic video surveillance to identify the people who regularly come and go and would also like to install silent video surveillance cameras inside her home. (1) Would installing a concealed video surveillance camera on the telephone pole across the street from Mary's home violate her rights under the Fourth Amendment? (2) Would sneaking into Mary's home while she is away and installing a concealed video surveillance camera inside her home violate Mary's rights under the Fourth Amendment? (3) Is there any way the Whosville Police Department may legitimately install a concealed video surveillance camera inside Mary's home? (§5.7)

15. What is a detection device? Give at least three examples. (§ 5.7)

16. What reason has the Supreme Court given for holding that a sniff performed by a trained narcotics detection dog does not involve a search? (§ 5.7)

17 Does requiring airline passengers to undergo magnetometer screening and have their carry-on luggage x-rayed before boarding a plane involve a search? Why are individualized suspicion and a search warrant not required? Explain both answers. (§ 5.7)

18. What three things are necessary under the Wiretap Act for an interception to occur? (§5.9)

19. What three kinds of communications are protected by the Wiretap Act? Which kind was involved in *Olmstead v. United States*? In *Katz v. United States*? (§§5.2, 5.4)

20. What is necessary for an *oral communication* to be protected under the Wiretap Act? (§5.9)

21. Mary Wanna's business has prospered and she now has an office with a waiting room and secretary. Officers Harris and West went to Mary's office and asked to speak with her. Mary's secretary announced their presence and returned, telling them they would have to wait a few minutes. She then departed for lunch. While sitting in Mary's waiting room, the officers noticed that a light on the secretary's extension phone was blinking. They picked up the extension phone and listened to Mary's telephone conversation. Did they violate the Wiretap Act? (§5.9)

22. The Wiretap Act provides strong protection for the privacy of communications. The procedures for obtaining and executing wiretap orders exceed Fourth Amendment requirements for conventional search warrants. Identify as many Wiretap Act procedural safeguards as you can. (§5.10)

23. What three areas of communications surveillance fall outside the scope of the Wiretap Act? (§§5.11-5.14)

24. Police officers rent a motel room adjoining Mary Wanna's room to conduct communication surveillance. Mary is cautious and speaks only in a whisper. Frustrated at not being able to hear, police place a stethoscope against the common wall and listen through the stethoscope. The stethoscope amplifies the sounds sufficiently so that the police are able to hear everything Mary whispers. Does this violate the Wiretap Act? (§§ 5.9, 5.12, 5.13)

25. The backseats of all Whosville Police Department squad cars are equipped with concealed microphones and tape recorders. Police arrested Mary Wanna and one of her associates during a drug bust, placed them in the backseat of a squad car, and took the long route to the police station. By the time the patrol car arrived at the police station, there was no need for a custodial interrogation. Mary had said it all. Did the Whosville Police Department violate Wiretap Act? (§ 5.13)

26. Which of the following examples falls within the consent exception to the Wiretap Act? (§ 5.14)
    a.   Judy Judas, a police informant, engages Mary Wanna in an incriminating conversation while wearing a concealed radio transmitter and tape recorder.

  b.   Judy Judas consents to allow the police tap her own telephone line so that
       they can monitor incoming calls.
  c.   Judy Judas consents to allow the police to listen on her extension phone
       while she places a call to Mary Wanna.
  d.   Mary Wanna, while in prison, calls Judy Judas and threatens her life for
       sending her to prison. Her call was monitored and recorded. There was a sign
       over the phone stating that calls made from prison phones are monitored.

28. When are e-mail, voice mail, and text messages protected by the Wiretap Act?
    The Stored Wire and Electronic Communications and Transactional Records
    Act? What is necessary to obtain access to e-mail during the first 180 days of
    storage? After 180 days? (§ 5.15)

29. What is a pen register device? A trap-and-trace device? What legal steps are
    required before installing and using them? (§5.16)

Chapter 6
Interrogations and Confessions

Objectives

Confessions provide powerful evidence of guilt. However, they are not admissible for this purpose if they are products of a police violation of a suspect's Fourth, Fifth, Sixth, or Fourteenth Amendment rights. This chapter discusses the interrogation requirements that stem from these four amendments. The main objective of this chapter is to instill an awareness and appreciation of what police must do and refrain from doing in order to procure an admissible confession. The student should emerge from this chapter with a thorough understanding of:

1. The kinds of interrogation practices that can lead to suppression of a confession under the free and voluntary requirement.

2. The impact of a police violation of a suspect's Fourth Amendment rights on the admissibility of a subsequent confession.

3. When the *Miranda* rule applies and what police must do to comply with the rule.

4. When the Sixth Amendment right to counsel applies and what must do (or refrain from doing) to comply with this requirement

Discussion Outline

§6.1   Introduction

    A. Grounds for excluding confessions. A confession is not admissible as evidence of guilt if it is the product of a police violation of any of the following requirements:

        1. Due process free and voluntary requirement;

        2. Fourth Amendment restrictions on investigatory stops, arrests, and searches;

3. *Miranda* rule which is designed to bolster protection for the Fifth Amendment privilege against self-incrimination during police custodial interrogations; and

4. Sixth Amendment right to counsel.

At one time, there was a fifth ground for excluding confessions called the *McNabb-Mallory* rule, but the force of this rule has been considerably muted in recent years.

B. Periods during which each of these requirements is in effect.

§6.2   The Free and Voluntary Rule

Confessions are inadmissible under the due process clause when they result from: (1) coercive pressures exerted by an agent of the government that (2) overcome the suspect's free will and induce him or her to make a statement that he or she would not otherwise have made.

A. Coercive pressures exerted by an agent of the government

For a confession to be considered involuntary in a due process sense, the coercive pressures that cause the confession must be exerted by an agent of the government. The due process clause is not violated when the pressures come from within or are imposed by private parties acting without government complicity. The following police interrogation practices are considered improperly coercive:

1. Physical force or threats of force.

2. False promises that the suspect will avoid prosecution, receive a lighter sentence, or some other favorable treatment if he or she confesses.

3. Psychological coercion, such as threatening to arrest innocent family members or take the suspect's children away.

a. Deceiving suspects about the strength of the evidence against them, such as telling them their fingerprints were found at the crime scene, their alibi was not confirmed, etc. is not considered improperly coercive.

B. Impact of interrogation methods on the suspect

If the interrogation methods used by the police are determined to have been improper, the court must then decide whether the suspect's free will was overcome.

1. Physical force or threats of force render a confession involuntary as a matter of law. No further inquiry will be made.

2. When the pressures are less extreme, two additional factors will be considered.

   a. The suspect's susceptibility to the pressures (i.e., his or her background, intelligence, education, prior experience with the criminal justice system, current physical and mental condition, ability to cope with stress, etc.), and

   b. The conditions under which the interrogation took place (i.e., location of the interrogation, the length, intensity, and frequency of the interrogation sessions, food and sleep deprivation, the intimidating presence of a large number of police officers, etc.).

3. *Arizona v. Fulminante*—Part II.

§6.3　Fourth Amendment Exclusionary Rule

The Fourth Amendment exclusionary rule requires courts to suppress confessions if they are: (1) causally connected (2) to a violation of the suspect's Fourth Amendment rights, such as a *Terry* stop, arrest, or search.

A.　Causal connection

Courts consider the following three factors in deciding whether a causal connection:

1. *Length of time between the Fourth Amendment violation and the confession.* Confessions given at the scene of a Fourth Amendment violation are always considered causally related.

2. *The presence of intervening circumstances.* Lapse of time alone is rarely sufficient to break the causal chain. Generally, there must be intervening circumstances indicating that the suspect's decision to confess was a deliberate act of free will. Consulting with family members or an attorney and voluntarily returning to the police station after being released are the two circumstances most often relied on to show this. Either is sufficient to break the causal chain and render a subsequent confession admissible.

3. *Purpose and flagrancy of the police violation.* The purpose and flagrancy of the violation are relevant to the policy behind the exclusionary rule, which is to deter police violations of the Fourth Amendment. Consequently, courts are more willing to find a break in the causal chain and admit the confession where the violation is unwitting and does not enable the police to obtain a confession they could not otherwise have obtained without the violation.

4. *Kaupp v. Texas*—Part II.

B. Derivative evidence

When a confession is tainted by a Fourth Amendment violation, the taint carries over and destroys the admissibility of derivative evidence, which would not have been discovered without the confession.

§6.4   Overview of the Rules Governing Custodial Interrogation

Two additional requirements go into effect once a suspect is placed under arrest or taken into custody: (1) prompt arraignment statutes, and (2) the *Miranda* rule.

§6.5   The *McNabb-Mallory* Delay in Arraignment Rule

Statement of the *McNabb-Mallory* rule. The *McNabb-Mallory* rule required federal courts to exclude confessions obtained during a period of "unnecessary delay" in taking the arrestee before a magistrate, even if the confession was otherwise voluntary.

A. Basis for the rule

The *McNabb-Mallory* rule was adopted by the Supreme Court to enforce compliance with Rule 5(a) of the Federal Rules of Criminal Procedure, which requires federal agents to take arrested persons before the nearest available magistrate, commissioner, or other committing officer for an arraignment "without unnecessary delay" following arrest.

B. Current status of the *McNabb-Mallory* rule in federal courts

The 1968 Omnibus Crime Control and Safe Streets Act (Part II) modified the *McNabb-Mallory* rule in the following ways:

1. It makes "voluntariness" the sole criterion for admissibility of confessions in federal courts. Unnecessary delay in taking an arrested person before a magistrate is reduced to a factor bearing on voluntariness, but not independent grounds for suppression.

2. This factor may only be considered for confessions given more than six hours after an arrest on federal charges. It may not be considered for confessions given within the first six hours after the arrest.

C. Status of the *McNabb-Mallory* rule in state courts

Because the Supreme Court promulgated the *McNabb-Mallory* rule under its supervisory authority over the federal courts, not as a rule of constitutional law, the rule was never binding on state courts. Most states treat unnecessary delay in arraignment as a factor in evaluating whether the arrestee's confession was voluntary, but not as independent grounds for suppressing confessions that are found to be voluntary.

§6.6 Protection for the Fifth Amendment Privilege Against Self-Incrimination During Police Interrogations:

The *Miranda* Rule

A. Statement of the *Miranda* rule

The *Miranda* rule is operative whenever police interrogate a suspect who is then in custody about an offense for which he or she has not yet been charged. To procure an admissible confession, police must:

1. warn the suspect of his or her Fifth Amendment rights,

2. secure a knowing, intelligent, and voluntary waiver before initiating questioning, and

3. cease interrogating if the suspect at any time thereafter manifests a desire to remain silent or to consult with an attorney.

   Violation of any of these duties will result in suppression of the confession.

B. Policy underlying the *Miranda* rule

The Supreme Court had three purposes in mind for establishing *Miranda* safeguards: (1) to aid suspects in asserting their Fifth Amendment privilege against self-incrimination during police custodial interrogations, (2) to ensure that the police do not practice coercion behind closed doors, and (3) to relieve the burden on courts of having to scrutinize individual cases, after the fact, to try to determine whether a particular confession was voluntary.

C. *Miranda v. Arizona*—Part II.

§6.7 Custodial Interrogation Defined

A. When the rule applies

Miranda safeguards are necessary only during custodial interrogations. For police/suspect interaction to be considered a custodial interrogation, two ingredients are necessary: custody and interrogation.

B. *Custody* defined

Custody exists when the interrogation environment has the coercive atmosphere of an arrest. Factors that can create an arrest-like atmosphere include: (1) prolonged questioning, (2) questioning in isolated surroundings, (3) the threatening presence of several police officers, (4) the display of weapons, (5) physical touching of the suspect, (6) a hostile or accusatory attitude toward the suspect, (7) intimidating language or tone of voice, (8) handcuffs or other physical restraints, and (9) confronting the suspect with evidence of guilt.

1. The suspect must be aware that the interrogator is a police officer for the interrogation environment to have the coercive atmosphere of an arrest.

2. Suspects are generally not in custody during routine traffic stops and many investigative stops because the objective circumstances surrounding these encounters rarely resemble an arrest.

   a. *Berkemer v. McCarty*—Part II.

C. *Interrogation* defined

   Miranda safeguards are necessary only when a suspect in custody is interrogated. Interrogation, for purposes of *Miranda* analysis, includes both express questioning and its functional equivalent. "Functional equivalent" refers to words or actions on the part of the police (other than those normally attendant to arrest and custody) that the police should know are reasonably likely to elicit an incriminating response from the suspect.

   1. Express questioning

      a. Statements volunteered without an interrogation are admissible despite lack of *Miranda* warnings.

      b. Warnings are not required before asking "routine booking questions," because the officer has no reason to expect that such questions will elicit an incriminating response from the suspect. See *Pennsylvania v. Muniz* (Part II; Chapter 7).

   2. Functional equivalent of express questioning

      a. Words or actions on the part of the police that they should know are reasonably likely to elicit an incriminating response from the suspect are considered the "functional equivalent" of express questioning and also trigger the need for *Miranda* safeguards. The functional equivalent prong is aimed at psychological ploys used to overcome a suspect's silence, such as telling him or her that he or she was implicated by a confederate, identified by an eyewitness, etc.

      b. *Rhode Island v. Innis*—Part II.

D. Public safety exception

1. The police may delay administration of *Miranda* warnings before interrogating a suspect in custody when they are confronted with an emergency that requires immediate action to protect the public safety or their own safety.

2. *Benson v. State*—Part II.

F. Non-police interrogators

Private detectives and security officers are not required to observe *Miranda* safeguards because the Constitution constrains only the actions of the government.

§6.8 Procedural Requirements for Custodial Interrogations: *Miranda* Warnings and Waivers

A. Warnings

Prior to interrogating a suspect who is in custody (but not yet under formal charges), police must issue the following set of warnings:

1. You have the right to remain silent.

2. If you do make a statement, anything you say can and will be used against you in court.

3. You have the right to consult with an attorney and have an attorney present during the questioning.

4. If you cannot afford an attorney, one will be appointed for you prior to any questioning if you so desire.

B. Waiver

After *Miranda* warnings have been administered, the officer must obtain a knowing, intelligent, and voluntary waiver of the suspect's *Miranda* rights before questioning may begin.

C. Cessation of questioning

Notwithstanding an initial waiver, the suspect remains free to assert the right to remain silent or to speak with an attorney at any point during the interview. After the suspect has made a clear and unambiguous assertion of either right, all questioning must cease immediately. Police are free to ignore ambiguous or equivocal assertions and are not required to ask clarifying questions. *Davis v. United States* (Part II).

D. Resumption of questioning after a suspect has clearly indicated the desire to remain silent or to speak with an attorney

1. After a suspect makes a clear and unambiguous request for an attorney, police may not thereafter question the suspect about any offense until counsel is present unless the suspect initiates further communication with the police.

2. After a suspect makes a clear and unambiguous assertion of the right to remain silent, police may not thereafter question the suspect about the same offense unless the suspect initiates further communication with the police. However, the police may initiate questioning about an unrelated offense, after waiting a sufficient period of time.

§6.9 Sixth Amendment Right to Counsel During Interrogations Conducted After Formal Charges are Filed

A. Attachment of the Sixth Amendment right to counsel

The Sixth Amendment right to the assistance of counsel attaches when adversary judicial proceedings are formally initiated by way of a preliminary hearing, indictment, information, or arraignment. An arrest, whether with or without a warrant, does not trigger protection of the Sixth Amendment right to counsel.

B. Policy behind Sixth Amendment restrictions on police questioning

The policy behind Sixth Amendment restrictions on questioning is to prevent the police from undermining the ability of defense counsel to mount an effective defense. Once the Sixth Amendment right to counsel has attached, police may not deliberately elicit incriminating statements pertaining to the charges at a time when counsel is not present unless the defendant gives a valid *waiver*. Valid waivers of the Sixth Amendment counsel are difficult to obtain. See §6.9(E) below.

C. Deliberate elicitation standard

Protection of the Sixth Amendment right to counsel is not confined to custodial interrogations. Once formal charges are filed, the Sixth Amendment entitles the defendant to the assistance and presence of counsel whenever the police *deliberately elicit* incriminating statements about the charges, whether the defendant is in custody, the verbal exchange constitutes an interrogation under *Miranda*, or the defendant is aware that the questioner is a police officer.

1. Undercover interrogations conducted after formal charges are lodged violate the Sixth Amendment right to counsel.

2. Active solicitation of information is necessary. A violation of the Sixth Amendment right to counsel does not occur by planting a police informant in the defendant's cell if the informant does nothing more than serve as a willing listener.

Kuhlmann v. Wilson—Part II.

D. Offense-Specific Nature of the Sixth Amendment right to counsel

    1. Sixth Amendment right to counsel is offense-specific, meaning that it applies only when police question a defendant under formal charges about *that* offense. It does not apply when their questions relate to uncharged criminal activity, even when crime under investigation is closely related factually to the one that is the subject of the charges.

    2. However, if the accused is in custody when questioned about uncharged criminal activity, such as where the accused is in jail awaiting trial on the charges, police must observe *Miranda* procedures.

E. Waiver of the Sixth Amendment right to counsel

    1. A valid waiver is necessary to obtain an admissible statement from a criminal defendant pertaining to the charges at a time when counsel is not present.

    2. Once a criminal defendant has retained counsel or requested appointment of counsel, the police cannot obtain a valid waiver of the Sixth Amendment right to counsel during an encounter with the defendant that they initiate. Statements made during a police-initiated encounter will be suppressed, even though the defendant agrees to discuss the charges and executes a written waiver.

        a. *Michigan v. Jackson*—Part II.

    3. A valid waiver of the Sixth Amendment right to counsel can be obtained outside the presence of counsel only if: (1) the accused initiates the encounter with the police or (2) the police initiate the counter *before* the accused has retained counsel or requested the court to appoint counsel. In instances where a valid waiver of rights is possible, administration of *Miranda* warnings provides an adequate advice of rights; there are no special Sixth Amendment warnings.

§6.10 Use of Inadmissible Confessions for Impeachment

A. An inadmissible confession may be used for impeachment only if the following conditions are met:

    1. The defendant decides to take the witness stand and testify at his or her trial.

    2. He or she tells the jurors a different story from the one he or she told the police.

    3. The confession was given voluntarily.

B. When a confession is admitted for impeachment purposes, the jurors may consider it only for the sake of evaluating the veracity of the defendant's inconsistent trial testimony. They may not consider the confession as evidence that the defendant is guilty of the crime confessed.

§6.11   Restrictions on the Use of Derivative Evidence

A. Confessions often lead to the discovery of other evidence. Evidence obtained as a result of the confession, such as physical evidence, witness leads, and later confessions, is called "derivative evidence."

B. Derivative evidence is inadmissible when a confession was obtained in violation of the due process free and voluntary requirement, the Fourth Amendment search and seizure clause, the Fifth Amendment privilege against self-incrimination, or the Sixth Amendment right to counsel.

C. *Miranda* warning violations do not require suppression of derivative evidence if the confession is voluntary and the violation was not deliberate.

1. *Missouri v. Seibert*—Part II.

§6.12   Restrictions on the Use of Confessions Given by Accomplices

A. A defendant may not object to admission of an accomplice's confession as evidence against him or her on the grounds it was unconstitutionally obtained. Only the person whose constitutional rights were violated may raise this objection.

B. However, the government may not use one accomplice's confession as evidence against another unless the accomplice who gave the confession appears at the latter's trial and testifies. The basis for this restriction is the Sixth Amendment guarantee that "[i]n all criminal prosecutions, the accused shall enjoy the right . . . to be confronted with the witnesses against him."

§6.13   The Requirement of Corroboration of Valid Confessions

A. Many states impose a statutory restriction on the admission of confessions called the *corpus delicti* or independent proof requirement. The prosecution must put on at least some evidence, independent of the confession, that the crime confessed was in fact committed before a confession will be received into evidence.

Review Questions

1. Confessions may be excluded from criminal trials if they are obtained in violation of an assortment of constitutional and statutory provisions. List the constitutional or statutory provisions and briefly describe the restriction each imposes. (§6.1)

2. Which of the five requirements discussed in this chapter are in effect during Phase 1 (investigative questioning of suspects who are not in custody)? (Figure 6.1)

3. Which of the five requirements discussed in this chapter are effect during Phase 2 (interrogation of suspects who are in police custody but have not yet been formally charged)? (Figure 6.1)

4. Which of the five requirements discussed in this chapter are in effect during Phase 3 (interrogations conducted after formal charges have been filed)? (Figure 6.1)

5. What is the justification for suppressing involuntary confessions? What two elements must combine for a confession to be suppressed under the free and voluntary requirement? Give several examples of improper forms of persuasion. What factors do courts consider in deciding whether improper police interrogation practices overcame the suspect's free will? (§6.2)

6. In a pretrial suppression hearing, which party has the burden of proof on the question of voluntariness? (§6.2)

7. The Fourth Amendment exclusionary rule requires suppression of confessions that are "causally connected" to a Fourth Amendment violation. What kinds of Fourth Amendment violations can cause a confession to be excluded? (§6.3)

8. What three factors do courts consider in deciding whether a confession given subsequent to a violation of the suspect's Fourth Amendment rights was "causally connected" to that violation? (§6.3)

9. If the confession is found to be "causally connected," what effect does this have on the admissibility of other evidence uncovered as a result of the confession ? (§6.3, 6.11)

10. Once a suspect has been placed under formal arrest or taken into custody, two new requirements go into effect. What are they? (§6.4)

11. State the *McNabb-Mallory* rule. What was the legal foundation on which the Supreme Court based this rule? What is its present status in federal courts? Was this rule binding on state courts? What is the present status of the *McNabb-Mallory* rule in state courts? (§6.5)

12. What conditions are necessary for the *Miranda* rule to apply? (§6.6, 6.7)

13. How is "custody" defined for *Miranda* purposes? What factors do courts considered in deciding whether a suspect, who has not yet been arrested, is in custody for warning purpose? (§6.7)

14. Are *Miranda* warnings required when a police undercover officer questions a suspect? Explain why or why not? (§6.7)

15. Are warnings required during routine traffic stops? During *Terry* stops? Explain why or why not? (§6.7)

16. Officer Nichols observed a vehicle speeding on the expressway, activated his siren, and then pulled the vehicle over. Nichols approached the vehicle, asked the driver, Frank Long, for his license and registration, and issued a citation for speeding. While speaking with Long, Nichols detected the odor of marijuana smoke inside the passenger compartment and asked Long and his two companions whether any of them had been smoking marijuana. When they denied this, Nichols asked for permission to search Long's vehicle. Long consented and he and his companions exited the vehicle, at Nichols' request. During the ensuing search, Nichols discovered a bag of marijuana on the floor behind the driver's seat and asked Long and his two companions which of them owned the marijuana. After a few minutes of silence, Long confessed to owning it. At his trial for possession of marijuana, Long moved to suppress his confession on the grounds that Officer Nichols failed to administer *Miranda* warnings before inquiring into ownership of the marijuana. Should the court suppress Long's confession? (§6.7)

17. How is "interrogation" defined for *Miranda* purposes? What is necessary for police words or actions, not involving an express question, to be considered its "functional equivalent?" Give several examples of police words or actions that constitute the functional equivalent of an express question. (§6.7)

18. Are warnings required before asking routine booking questions? (§ 6.7)

19. What conditions are necessary for the "public safety" exception to the *Miranda* rule to apply? Give an example of a situation in which this exception would apply. (§6.7)

20. Who besides police officers are required to give *Miranda* warnings? (§6.7)

21. Recite the four warnings required by the *Miranda* rule. Must the warnings be given in the exact language laid down by the Supreme Court in *Miranda* in order to be effective? (§6.8)

22. What is necessary for an effective waiver of *Miranda* rights? Discuss. (§6.8)

23. What is necessary to obligate the police to cease questioning after a suspect has made a valid waiver of *Miranda* rights and questioning has begun? (§6.8)

24. Under what conditions, if any, may police resume questioning after the suspect has made a clear and unambiguous request to speak with an attorney? (§6.8)

25. Under what conditions, if any, may police resume questioning of a suspect after the suspect has clearly indicated a wish to remain silent? (§6.8)

26. When does the Sixth Amendment right to counsel attach? (§6.9)

27. What is the policy behind Sixth Amendment restrictions on police questioning? (§6.9)

28. Under what circumstances, if any, may the police question a defendant under formal charges about that offense at a time when counsel is not present? Discuss. (§6.9)

29. When, if ever, can the police obtain a valid waiver of the Sixth Amendment right to counsel during an encounter that they initiate? That the defendant initiates? In those situations where obtaining a valid waiver is possible, what must police do to obtain one? (§6.9)

30. The *Miranda* and the Sixth Amendment right to counsel differ in a number of ways. State them. (§6.9)

31. What does use of a confession "for impeachment" mean? What three conditions are necessary for the prosecution to use an inadmissible confession for this purpose? May the prosecution use a confession procured in violation of the *Miranda* rule for impeachment? In violation of the Sixth Amendment right to counsel? In violation of the due process free and voluntary requirement? (§6.10)

32. What is derivative evidence? (§6.11)

33. When may the prosecutor use of evidence uncovered through a confession obtained in violation of the: (1) due process free and voluntary requirement? (2) Fourth Amendment search and seizure clause, (3) *Miranda* rule? (4) Sixth Amendment right to counsel? (§6.11)

34. What is the constitutional basis for a defendant's objection to the government use of an accomplice's confession against him or her?

35. What is the *corpus delicti* requirement? (§6.13)

Chapter 7
Compulsory Self-Incrimination

Objectives

This chapter discusses Fifth and Fourth Amendment limitations on the government's power to compel citizens to furnish self-incriminating evidence. The Fifth Amendment is concerned with testimonial self-incrimination (i.e., compulsion to disclose one's private thoughts). Its application during custodial interrogations was discussed in Chapter 6. This chapter provides a more complete analysis of the Fifth Amendment. The second limitation stems from the Fourth Amendment prohibition of unreasonable searches and seizures. Evidence taken from a suspect's body is called physical evidence. Compulsory production of self-incriminating physical evidence requires a restriction of the suspect's freedom of movement (i.e., a seizure of his or her person) and sometimes also an invasion of his or her privacy or bodily integrity. Concern for these interests is addressed by the Fourth Amendment. This chapter builds on the Fourth Amendment principles introduced in Chapters 3 and 4. The student should leave this chapter with an understanding of:

1. The constitutional principles that regulate compulsory production of self-incriminating testimonial and physical evidence;

2. The range of proceedings in which protection of the Fifth Amendment privilege against self-incrimination may be invoked, and how it is invoked and waived;

3. The requirements needed to trigger protection of the privilege against self-incrimination: compulsion, testimony, and self-incrimination.

4. The distinction between appearance evidence and bodily evidence and the range of police procedures that involve each;

5. Fourth Amendment requirements for compulsory production of appearance evidence;

6. Fourth Amendment requirements for highly intrusive bodily searches (i.e., searches that penetrate the body surface, result in extraction of bodily tissues or fluids, or involve significant pain, physical discomfort, or humiliation), including when a search warrant is required and when it is excused by exigent circumstances; and

7. Fourth Amendment requirements for strip and body cavity searches.

Discussion Outline

§ 7.1   Introduction

    A.   Self-incriminating evidence is divided into two categories—testimony and physical evidence.

        1.   Testimony encompasses any behavior that explicitly or implicitly makes a statement or discloses information. The source of constitutional protection against compelled disclosure of a person's thoughts is the Fifth Amendment, which declares that "[n]o person . . . shall be compelled in any criminal case to be a witness against himself."

        2.   Physical evidence includes all evidence other than testimony. A suspect's body can be the source of two different kinds of physical evidence—appearance evidence and bodily evidence. The source of constitutional protection against compelled production of physical evidence is the Fourth Amendment.

§ 7.2   Fifth Amendment Protection against Testimonial Self-Incrimination

    A.   The Fifth Amendment privilege against testimonial self-incrimination is violated whenever the government compels disclosure of information that could later be used against the person in a criminal proceeding. The self-incrimination clause of the Fifth Amendment applies both inside and outside the courtroom and in all legal proceedings, civil or criminal, formal or informal.

    B.   There are two degrees of Fifth Amendment protection.

        1.   Citizens enjoy an absolute right to remain silent during custodial interrogations and at their criminal trial.

        2.   In all other situations, they may be compelled to appear and testify, but are privileged to refuse to answer specific questions if the answer might tend to incriminate them.

            a.   *Illustration.* A and B are arrested on charges of operating a drug trafficking ring and taken to the police station for interrogation. Both have a Fifth Amendment right to remain silent (i.e., to refuse to participate in the interrogation). A is tried first and B is subpoenaed to testify at A's trial. A has a right to remain silent (i.e., to refuse to take the witness stand) at his trial. B does not have this right; B must appear and take the witness stand in response to a subpoena, and must answer all questions put to him except those that call for an incriminating response. If the prosecutor asks "Did you and A conspire to traffic in drugs?" B may invoke the Fifth Amendment and refuse to answer.

§ 7.3   Prerequisites for Application of the Fifth Amendment

Three prerequisites are necessary to trigger the protection of the Fifth Amendment privilege against self-incrimination: (1) testimony, (2) compulsion, and (3) self-incrimination.

A. *Testimony*. Testimony, for purposes of the Fifth Amendment, includes any behavior that, implicitly or explicitly, makes a statement or communicates thoughts or information.

B. *Compulsion*. Compulsion occurs when the government threatens a serious consequence unless the person makes a statement or furnishes information. The threatened consequences may take the form of contempt sanctions for disobeying a subpoena, physical retaliation, job loss, or any other serious harm.

   1. The relevant time for evaluating whether a person has been compelled to incriminate himself or herself in violation of the Fifth Amendment is when the incriminating statement is originally made. The Fifth Amendment does not protect a person's voluntarily prepared private papers from seizure under a search warrant because the element of compulsion to make the self-incriminating statement is lacking.

      a. *United States v. Hubbell*

C. *Self-Incrimination*. To be self-incriminating, the statement must expose the maker to risk of criminal prosecution.

   1. Persons under arrest may be compelled to furnish biographical information (i.e., name, address, Social Security number, etc.) needed for booking, because this information is not incriminating.

   2. Persons who have already been tried for the crime to which the questions relate may not invoke protection of the Fifth Amendment, because the double jeopardy clause will prevent the government from prosecuting them again.

   3. Persons who have been granted immunity from prosecution may not invoke the protection of the Fifth Amendment.

      a. Two different kinds of immunity are available: absolute immunity and use (including derivative use) immunity.

§ 7.4   Rules for Invoking and Waiving Fifth Amendment Protections

A. Invoking the Fifth Amendment

   1. Criminal defendants have a Fifth Amendment right to remain silent at their criminal trial. They invoke this right by not taking the witness stand. The prosecution may not call the defendant as a witness.

2. Witnesses other than criminal defendants do not have the right to remain silent. They must take the witness stand and be sworn in, and may invoke the privilege only if they are asked a question that calls for an incriminating response.

B. Waiving the privilege

1. A waiver occurs when a person who has a Fifth Amendment privilege voluntarily testifies without invoking it. Under *Miranda*, a valid waiver requires a warning that the person is not required to answer, etc. However, the Supreme Court has declined to impose a similar requirement in other contexts.

2. Criminal defendants who take the witness stand waive the privilege, but only concerning the matters about which they have testified. They retain the right to invoke the privilege if they are cross-examined about matters beyond the scope of their testimony.

§ 7.5   Protection against Adverse Consequences from Exercising the Privilege against Self-Incrimination

A. Judges and prosecutors are not permitted to make adverse comments about a defendant's refusal to answer police questions during a custodial interrogation or a defendant's decision not to testify at his or her criminal trial or sentencing hearing.

B. Adverse inferences may be drawn about a person's assertion of the Fifth Amendment privilege in other legal proceedings, including civil trials, parole revocation hearings, and police disciplinary actions. Although witnesses are permitted to invoke the privilege in these proceedings, the Fifth Amendment does not guarantee that their decision to do so will be cost-free.

§ 7.6   Self-Reporting Laws and the Fifth Amendment

A. The Fifth Amendment does not privilege a person to refuse to file a required report that could draw attention to his or her criminal activity when the reporting requirement furthers a legitimate regulatory purpose.

1. The Internal Revenue Code, occupational tax laws, and hit-and-run motorist statutes are examples of some of the many statutes that impose reporting requirements that serve a legitimate regulatory purpose.

2. However, citizens may refuse to comply with government reporting laws that serve no regulatory purpose other than forcing them to disclose their criminal activity.

§ 7.7   Fourth Amendment Protection against Bodily Self-Incrimination

A.   The Fifth Amendment only protects an accused against being compelled to furnish self-incriminating testimony (i.e., to disclose his or her private thoughts). Evidence that derives from a suspect's body rather than his or her mind is called physical evidence. The Fifth Amendment affords no protection against compulsion to furnish self-incriminating physical evidence.

  1.   *Schmerber v. California*—Part II

  2.   *Pennsylvania v. Muniz*—Part II

B.   Compelled production of self-incriminating physical evidence is regulated by the Fourth Amendment. The Fourth Amendment protects three discrete interests people have in their bodies: (1) freedom of movement, (2) bodily privacy, and (3) bodily integrity. Concentrating on these three interests is the key to understanding Fourth Amendment protection against compulsory production of physical evidence. Freedom of movement is always implicated when the police perform procedures that require use of the suspect's body. This means that the police always need grounds for a seizure. Whether they need grounds beyond this depends on whether the procedures subsequently performed invade the suspect's privacy or bodily integrity. When police perform procedures that invade privacy or bodily integrity, they must have separate grounds for the second invasion as well.

C.   Physical evidence taken from a suspect's body is divided into two categories—appearance evidence and bodily evidence.

  1.   Appearance evidence refers to evidence derived from body characteristics that are routinely displayed to the public.

  2.   Bodily evidence refers to physical evidence obtained by searching areas of a suspect's body not normally exposed to the public, penetrating the body surface, or removing biological or foreign substances.

§ 7.8   Requirements for Appearance Evidence

A.   The most common police procedures involving appearance evidence are: (1) stationhouse lineups; (2) showup identifications at the crime scene; (3) photographing, measuring, fingerprinting, and taking handwriting and voice exemplars; and (4) field sobriety tests.

B.   Because the suspect's interest in freedom of movement is the only interest invaded by these procedures, compulsory production of appearance evidence is permitted whenever the police have constitutional grounds to seize the suspect and detain him or her long enough to perform the procedure.

1.   A lawful arrest carries the authority to compel participation in all appearance evidence procedures, without limitation.

2.   Police are more limited during *Terry* stops. Appearance evidence procedures that can be completed quickly in the field are permitted. Transporting a *Terry* detainee a short distance to a crime scene or to the location of a witness for a showup identification is also permitted. However, procedures such as lineups, which require transporting a detainee to the police station, are not allowed.

C.   Some jurisdictions have statutes authorizing the prosecutor to apply to a court for an order compelling suspects to appear on their own and participate in nontestimonial identification procedures. Covered procedures normally include lineups and fingerprinting, and furnishing handwriting, hair, blood, saliva, and urine samples.

D.   An illegal arrest taints appearance evidence. Fingerprint and footprint matches, positive lineup identifications, and other forms of appearance evidence derived from the illegal arrest will be suppressed.

§ 7.9   Requirements for Bodily Evidence

A.   Bodily evidence refers to evidence derived from a suspect's body by: (1) searching areas not normally exposed to the public, (2) penetrating the body surface, or (3) removing biological or foreign substances.

B.   The following procedures involve bodily evidence: (1) removing incriminating residue from the body's surface, (2) taking X-rays, (3) taking body tissue and fluids (i.e., blood, semen, urine, etc.) for forensic analysis, (4) performing strip searches and body cavity searches, and (5) reaching into a suspect's mouth or pumping his or her stomach to recover evidence.

C.   Unlike appearance evidence, which involves no intrusion beyond an interference with the suspect's freedom of movement, procedures involving bodily evidence either intrude on bodily privacy, resulting in a Fourth Amendment search, or involve removal of body tissues, fluids, or other materials, resulting in a Fourth Amendment seizure. Accordingly, the search and seizure principles discussed in Chapter 4 apply to procedures that involve bodily evidence.

1.   *Schmerber v. California*—Part II

2.   Intrusive bodily procedures may be performed to retrieve evidence only when: (1) The government's need for the evidence is greater than the intrusion into the suspect's privacy or bodily integrity required to obtain it; (2) There is a "clear indication" that the needed evidence is present or, stated another way, police have probable cause to believe that the procedure will be effective in producing the needed evidence; (3) Police either obtain a search

warrant or are excused from doing so by the exigent circumstances exception; (4) The procedure used to recover the evidence is reasonable and is performed in a reasonable manner (which often requires use of medically trained professionals).

3. Of all procedures, surgical intrusions under general anesthesia are the most invasive. In *Winston v. Lee*, the Supreme Court held that the prosecutor could not compel a robbery suspect to undergo a surgical operation under general anesthesia to remove a bullet from his body for use as evidence because the government's need for the evidence was not great enough to justify placing the defendant's life at risk.

§ 7.10   —Necessity of a Search Warrant to Explore for Bodily Evidence

A. Unless confronted with an emergency that threatens destruction of evidence, police should obtain a search warrant before arranging for procedures that involve: (1) taking saliva, urine, semen, pubic hair, or other bodily tissue or fluids; (2) penetration of the body's surface; (3) examination of rectal or genital cavities; (4) medical risk; or (5) significant pain, discomfort, or humiliation.

B. Exigent circumstances exception. The exigent circumstances exception excuses the need for a search warrant before searching for bodily evidence when police have probable cause to believe that incriminating evidence is present and that the evidence will be destroyed if they delay action to obtain a search warrant. Courts have applied this exception to:

1. Extracting blood to run tests for alcohol intoxication.

2. Swabbing for residue.

3. Retrieving swallowed evidence.

   a. *State v. Tapp*—Part II

§ 7.11   —Strip Searches and Body Cavity Searches

A. Strip searches (compulsory disrobing followed by a methodical visual inspection of the suspect's naked body) and manual body cavity searches (touching or probing of rectal or genital cavities) are not routine searches; they require additional justification beyond grounds for arrest. Strip searches require reasonable suspicion that the search will turn up evidence of drugs, weapons, or contraband. Because manual body cavity searches intrude inside the body, compliance with the requirements set forth in *Schmerber* is necessary.

Review Questions

1. Which amendment is concerned with the compulsion to provide self-incriminating testimony? What does that amendment provide? (§ 7.1)

2. Which amendment is concerned with bodily self-incrimination? (§ 7.1)

3. The Fifth Amendment provides that "[n]o person . . . shall be compelled in any *criminal* case to be a witness against himself." In what settings other than criminal trials can protection of the Fifth Amendment privilege against self-incrimination be invoked? Discuss. (§ 7.2)

4. What is the principal difference between the right to remain silent and the privilege not to answer incriminating questions? (§ 7.2)

5. In what legal contexts do citizens enjoy the right to remain silent? The privilege not to answer incriminating questions? (§ 7.2)

6. What three requirements are necessary to trigger protection of the Fifth Amendment privilege against self-incrimination? (§ 7.3)

7. How is the term *testimony* defined for purposes of the Fifth Amendment? (§ 7.3(A))

8. How is the term *compelled* defined for purposes of the Fifth Amendment? (§ 7.3(B))

9. What is necessary for a statement to be considered "self-incriminating"? (§ 7.3(C))

10. Indicate whether the Fifth Amendment privilege against self-incrimination is violated by any of the following procedures and explain why or why not.

    _____   a. Seizing a suspect's personal diary under a search warrant and using the incriminating statements contained in it as evidence against him or her. (§ 7.3(B))

    _____   b. Using a subpoena duces tecum to compel the target of a grand jury investigation to produce self-incriminating books and records. (§ 7.3(B))

    _____   c. Requiring a person under arrest to answer booking questions. (§ 7.3(C))

    _____   d. Requiring a person under arrest to appear in a lineup. (§§ 7.3(A), 7.7, 7.8)

    _____   e. Requiring a person under arrest to appear in a lineup and repeat two phrases that the robber is reputed to have said: "This is a holdup," and "Put all the money in a bag." (§§ 7.3(A), 7.7, 7.8)

    _____   f. Requiring a defendant at his criminal trial to take the witness stand and repeat words spoken during a secretly taped telephone conversation between the defendant and a police informant to enable the jury to compare the defendant's voice with the voice on the taped telephone conversation and determine whether the voice on the taped telephone conversation is his. (§§ 7.3(A), 7.7, 7.8)

11. Indicate whether Sam enjoys the right to remain silent, the privilege not to answer the specific question asked, or neither privilege, in each of the following situations. (§§ 7.2, 7.3)

————— a. Sam is arrested for driving under the influence of alcohol, taken to the police station, and asked questions about his name, address, Social Security number, date of birth, height, and weight for purposes of booking.

————— b. Sam is arrested for driving under the influence of alcohol and taken to the police station where he is questioned about whether he has been drinking.

————— c. Sam is subpoenaed to appear before a federal grand jury investigating whether he is guilty of tax evasion.

————— d. Sam is subpoenaed to appear before a federal grand jury investigating whether his sister Mary is guilty of tax evasion.

12. In what situations can a witness be compelled to provide testimony that concerns his or her own criminal activity? What are they? (§ 7.3(C))

13. What is the difference between absolute immunity and use (including derivative use) immunity? (§ 7.3(C))

14. Do police have the authority to offer either form of immunity to suspects in exchange for their voluntary cooperation in an interrogation? (§ 7.3(C))

15. How is the privilege against self-incrimination invoked by a defendant at his or her criminal trial? How is the privilege against self-incrimination invoked by a witness who is not the defendant? (§ 7.4)

16. When, if ever, can a defendant be questioned by the prosecutor at his or her criminal trial? (§ 7.4(C))

17. When, if ever, may the prosecutor comment on the accused's failure to testify at his or her criminal trial? (§ 7.5)

18. Does the Fifth Amendment exempt citizens engaged in criminal activity from filing mandatory government reports that could call attention to their criminal activity? Explain. (§ 7.6)

19. What protection does the Fifth Amendment provide against the government's use of a suspect's body to obtain evidence? (§§ 7.1, 7.7, 7.8(A); *Schmerber v. California* (Part II)).

20. George was arrested and taken to the police station, where he was given a field sobriety test during which he was required to raise one foot approximately six inches off the ground and, while in that position and looking at that foot, to count backwards from 40 to 1. George made numerous mistakes, supporting the inference that he was too intoxicated to perform the task. At his trial, George moved to suppress evidence of his performance on the field sobriety test on the grounds that the evidence was obtained in violation of his Fifth Amendment privilege against

self-incrimination. The trial judge denied George's motion. Why? (§§ 7.3(A), 7.7, 7.8(A); *Schmerber v. California* (Part II); *Pennsylvania v. Muniz* (Part II)).

21. Must *Miranda* warnings be administered before compelling a suspect to submit to the following procedures? Explain why or why not:
    a.   Fingerprinting
    b.   Photographing
    c.   Providing a handwriting specimen
    d.   Participating in a lineup
    (§§ 7.7, 7.8(A); *Schmerber v. California* (Part II); *Pennsylvania v. Muniz* (Part II).

22. The Fourth Amendment protects three distinct interests that citizens have in their bodies. Identify them. (§ 7.7)

23. What is appearance evidence? What is bodily evidence? Which of the three interests protected by the Fourth Amendment does compelled participation in appearance evidence procedures invade? What of the three interests protected by the Fourth Amendment does compelled participation in bodily evidence procedures invade? (§§ 7.7, 7.8)

24. Classify the following procedures in terms of whether they involve appearance evidence or bodily evidence:
    a.   Photographing?
    b.   Participation in a lineup?
    c.   Strip searches?
    d.   Compulsory submission of a handwriting sample?
    e.   Compulsory submission of a semen sample?
    f.   Drawing blood?
    g.   Fingerprinting?
    h.   Performing a field sobriety test?
    i.   Swabbing incriminating residue from under a suspect's fingernails?
    j.   Reaching into a suspect's mouth to prevent him or her from swallowing evidence? (§§ 7.7, 7.8, 7.9)

25. What Fourth Amendment requirements must be satisfied before police may compel suspects to participate in appearance evidence procedures? (§ 7.8)

26. What appearance evidence procedures may police perform during a *Terry* stop? Explain. (§ 7.8(C))

27. What does the Fourth Amendment normally require before police may compel suspects to furnish bodily evidence? (§ 7.9)

28. Is a search warrant always necessary before compelling a subject to furnish bodily evidence? Explain. (§ 7.10)

29. What is a strip search? What is a manual body cavity search? What Fourth Amendment requirements must be satisfied before performing a strip search? A manual body cavity search? (§ 7.11)

Chapter 8
Right to Counsel

Objectives

This chapter covers the Sixth Amendment right to counsel and constitutional restrictions on pretrial witness identification. There are three segments. The first segment covers the main features of the Sixth Amendment right to counsel. The second discusses the restrictions that the Sixth Amendment right to counsel imposes on the police. The last segment deals with Fourth, Fifth, Sixth, and Fourteenth Amendment restrictions on pretrial witness identification.

After completing this chapter, the student should emerge with a working knowledge of:

1. The four main features of the Sixth Amendment right to counsel, namely: (1) the right of indigent defendants to appointment of counsel, (2) the right to counsel in pretrial and post-trial proceedings, (3) the defendant's right of self-representation, and (4) the minimum standards for effective assistance of counsel.

2. Sixth Amendment restrictions on the conduct of the police, including:
    a. Pretrial encounters during which the accused is entitled to have a lawyer present;
    b. Precautions police must take to secure a valid waiver of the Sixth Amendment right to counsel;
    c. An officer's obligation to secure appointed counsel for defendants who cannot afford a lawyer;
    d. The degree to which police must permit defense attorneys to play an active role during police procedures in which the defendant has a right to have a lawyer present;
    e. Conduct considered to be an improper intrusion into the attorney-client relationship.

3. Constitutional restrictions on the conduct of pretrial witness identification imposed by:
    a. The Sixth Amendment right to counsel,
    b. Fourth Amendment search and seizure clause, and
    c. Fifth and Fourteenth Amendment due process clauses.

Discussion Outline

§ 8.1   Overview of the Sixth Amendment Right to Counsel

    A.   The Sixth Amendment guarantees that "[i]n all criminal prosecutions, the accused shall enjoy the right . . . to have the assistance of counsel for his defense."

    B.   The right to counsel performs two functions that are extremely important to our adversary system of criminal justice:

        1.   It reduces the risk that innocent people will be convicted because they lack the legal skills necessary to put forth an effective defense.

        2.   It aids assertion of the other constitutional rights developed for the protection of criminal defendants.

§ 8.2   The Indigent Person's Right to Assistance of Counsel

    A.   The right of indigent defendants to assistance of counsel has developed in four stages.

        1.   For the first 150 years, the Sixth Amendment right to counsel was interpreted to mean only that the government could not deny defendants who had the means to hire a lawyer the right to assistance of counsel. It imposed no obligation on the government to furnish counsel to defendants who lacked the means to hire an attorney.

        2.   In *Powell v. Alabama*, the Supreme Court ruled that state courts were required to provide court-appointed counsel for indigent criminal defendants charged with a felony who were illiterate or otherwise handicapped in defending themselves. This duty stemmed from the Fourteenth Amendment due process obligation of state governments to afford criminal defendants the right to a fair trial.

        3.   Six years later, the Supreme Court ruled that federal courts were required to provide court-appointed counsel for *all* criminal defendants charged with a felony who lacked the means to hire a lawyer. The duty of federal courts to appoint counsel for indigent criminal defendants was grounded in the Sixth Amendment right to counsel.

        4.   In *Gideon v. Wainwright*, the Supreme Court ruled that the Sixth Amendment right to counsel was applicable to the states through incorporation into the Fourteenth Amendment and obligates state courts to provide court-appointed counsel to indigent criminal defendants charged with a felony, without regard to whether they are illiterate or otherwise disadvantaged in representing themselves.

           a.   *Gideon v. Wainwright*—Part II

B. Although the Sixth Amendment declares that the accused shall enjoy the right to counsel "in all criminal prosecutions," the Supreme Court has carved out an exception for misdemeanor prosecutions in which a fine alone is imposed. The Sixth Amendment does not require appointment of counsel for indigent defendants charged with misdemeanors unless they are actually sentenced to prison. Indigent defendants cannot be deprived of their liberty unless court-appointed counsel is made available to them, but they may be fined without the benefit of counsel.

§ 8.3   The Right to Assistance of Counsel in Non-Trial Proceedings: Critical Stages of the Prosecution

A. The right to counsel originally meant the right to have counsel present only at the trial. Supreme Court decisions during the past 50 years have steadily expanded the number of proceedings for which an accused has the right to have counsel present. An accused today has the right to have counsel present during any pretrial proceeding that constitutes a "critical stage" of the prosecution, as well as during the trial itself. To be considered a critical stage, a legal encounter must possess the following characteristics:

1. It must take place *after* the government has initiated prosecution.

   a. This limitation stems from the language of the Sixth Amendment, which guarantees the "accused" the right to assistance of counsel in "all criminal prosecutions." A suspect does not become an "accused" until a prosecution has been initiated. This is when the Sixth Amendment right to counsel attaches.

   b. Initiation occurs when the government commits itself to prosecute. Courts have identified several pretrial events that can signal the initiation of a prosecution:

      i.   the return of a grand jury indictment;

      ii. the filing of an information by a prosecutor; or

      iii. the arraignment of the defendant on an arrest warrant or a formal criminal complaint.

2. The encounter must involve a trial-like "confrontation" between the accused and the government.

3. The encounter must be of such a nature that important rights might be lost or a fair trial jeopardized if the defendant is forced to proceed without counsel being present. Defendants, for example, are entitled to have counsel present during post-prosecution lineups because they are entitled to challenge the admission of witness identification testimony at the trial if the lineup is conducted in

an impermissibly suggestive manner. It is necessary for counsel to observe the procedure to determine whether grounds exist for a challenge.

    a.   The following have been recognized as critical stage events:

        i.   *Court appearances*: bail hearings, preliminary hearings, arraignments, and sentencing hearings.

        ii.   *Pretrial investigative encounters*: interrogations, lineups, and showups conducted after the Sixth Amendment right to counsel has attached (i.e., after initiation of prosecution). Section 8.6(A) of this outline discusses when prosecution is initiated. The Sixth Amendment right to counsel does not apply to police/suspect encounters conducted before initiation of prosecution. Protection of the *Miranda* Fifth Amendment right to counsel is available during pre-prosecution custodial interrogations, but there is no right to counsel—Fifth or Sixth Amendment—during pre-prosecution lineups and showups.

  B. The Sixth Amendment right to counsel also applies to post-conviction sentencing proceedings and to the defendant's first appeal of the conviction or sentence.

§ 8.4   The Defendant's Right to Self-Representation

  A. The Sixth Amendment also guarantees criminal defendants the opposite right—the right to waive assistance of counsel and engage in self-representation. Before accepting a waiver, the trial judge has the obligation to make sure that the defendant is mentally competent and that his or her decision has been knowingly and intelligently made.

§ 8.5   Ineffective Assistance of Counsel

  A. The Sixth Amendment guarantees the right to *effective* assistance of counsel.

    1. This guarantee applies both to retained and appointed counsel.

    2. To secure the reversal of a conviction based on ineffective assistance of counsel, the defendant must demonstrate that: (1) counsel's representation was grossly deficient, not simply below average, and (2) but for counsel's errors, there is a reasonable probability that the outcome of the proceedings would have been different (i.e., that the defendant would have been acquitted or received a lighter sentence).

§ 8.6   Sixth Amendment Restrictions on the Conduct of the Police

A. The Sixth Amendment right to counsel automatically attaches with the initiation of prosecution and brings with it several restrictions on police interactions with the defendant. From this point forward, all lineups, showups, and other police-initiated contacts must be conducted in accordance with the following rules.

  1. If the defendant has already retained or requested appointment of counsel, police may not conduct a lineup or showup or initiate an interrogation relating to the pending charges unless the defendant's attorney is present. Waiver of the Sixth Amendment right to counsel during a police-initiated contact is invalid. (*Michigan v. Jackson*, Part II).

  2. If the defendant has not yet retained or requested appointment of counsel, police may initiate contact, but must either secure a knowing and voluntary waiver of the right to counsel or wait until counsel is present before proceeding.

      a. Voluntary participation after receiving *Miranda*-type warnings will suffice to waive the Sixth Amendment right to counsel.

      b. Special precautions should be taken in securing a waiver of the right to counsel from a juvenile. The juvenile's parent or guardian should be present or, if unavailable, counsel should be provided to assist the juvenile in making this decision.

      c. If the defendant invokes the right to counsel after being warned, the proceeding must be postponed until counsel is present.

  3. The degree to which police must permit counsel to participate depends on the procedure.

      a. During lineups and showups, counsel is entitled to observe, but nothing more.

      b. During pretrial interrogations, counsel is entitled to object to questions, instruct the accused not to answer, and even advise the accused to terminate the interrogation.

B. Once adversary judicial proceedings are initiated, the Sixth Amendment right to counsel imposes a continuing duty on the police to abstain from intruding into the confidentiality of the attorney-client relationship. Information uncovered by deliberate intrusions into the attorney-client relationship will be suppressed. Further, if the government's activity is particularly egregious and causes irreparable prejudice to the defendant's ability to defend, the court may even dismiss the charges.

  1. *State v. Quattlebaum*—Part II

§ 8.7   Pretrial Identification Procedures

A. Police use three pretrial identification procedures:

1. Photographic identifications—the witness is shown pictures of the suspect, either singly or as part of a photospread. The main use of photographic identification is to narrow the focus of an investigation in cases in which the witness and police are uncertain of the offender's identity.

2. Showups—the suspect is presented alone to an eyewitness for identification. The main use for showups is to confirm that the police have apprehended the "right person" in cases in which swift action is necessary.

3. Lineups—the suspect is exhibited, along with stand-ins who possess similar physical traits, to the witness for identification. The main use of lineups is to confirm that the police have apprehended the right person when police are not in a rush.

B. All three witness identification procedures, when properly conducted, generate evidence that is admissible at the trial.

C. Objections to the admissibility of pretrial identification testimony may be raised under four separate constitutional provisions—the Fourth Amendment search and seizure clause, the Fifth and Fourteenth Amendment due process clauses, and the Sixth Amendment right to counsel.

§ 8.8   Fourth Amendment Requirements for Pretrial Identification

A. Evidence of a positive pretrial identification will be suppressed if it derives from an illegal arrest or detention. Illustration: Police arrest Sam without probable cause and put him in a lineup, during which the victim identifies him. The victim's testimony concerning the line-up identification will be suppressed under the Fourth Amendment exclusionary rule.

B. A lawful arrest carries with it the authority, as a matter of course and with no further justification, to compel participation in lineups and showups.

C. While showups are permitted during *Terry* stops, lineups are not because police are not permitted to take *Terry* detainees to the police station. Because lineups are conducted at the stationhouse, they are beyond the scope of a *Terry* stop.

§ 8.9   Due Process Requirements for Pretrial Identification Procedures

A. The due process clause forbids admission of pretrial identification testimony obtained under circumstances that are *so unnecessarily suggestive as to create a substantial likelihood of misidentification*. This test has two parts: A defendant who seeks to suppress evidence of a positive pretrial identification must prove that: (1) the identification procedure was unnecessarily suggestive, and that (2) the unnecessary suggestiveness created a substantial risk of misidentification.

1. *Unnecessarily suggestive procedure.* Unnecessary suggestiveness can result either because the police: (1) select an identification procedure (usually a showup) that is unnecessarily suggestive under the circumstances, or (2) conduct an appropriate procedure in an unnecessarily suggestive manner.

   a. Showups are the most inherently suggestive of the three identification procedures because only one person is presented to the witness for identification and that person is in police custody; these two factors combine to communicate the message that the police think the person presented for identification is the culprit.

   b. Police should not use a showup unless: (1) the showup takes place close in time to the crime and (2) police have a strong need for a quick confirmation that they have apprehended the right person.

   c. Unnecessary suggestiveness can also be injected by the manner in which a witness identification procedure is conducted. Police should avoid the following practices during witness identification procedures: (1) telling the witness whom the police suspect or whom to choose, (2) displaying a single photograph in a photographic identification, (3) showing multiple pictures of a particular person in a photographic spread, (4) placing the suspect in a lineup with "grossly dissimilar" individuals; (5) placing the suspect in a lineup when the suspect alone is made to wear distinctive clothing allegedly worn by the perpetrator; (6) telling the witness that the culprit has been caught and then bringing the suspect alone before the witness or allowing the suspect to be viewed in jail; (7) placing the suspect in a lineup after the police have pointed the suspect out to the witness before the lineup; and (8) asking the participants in the lineup to try on a piece of clothing that fits only the suspect.

2. *Substantial risk of misidentification.* The second prong of the test requires the court to examine the surrounding circumstances to determine whether the unnecessary suggestiveness of the identification procedure created a substantial risk of a mistaken identification. Flawed procedures do not necessarily mean that a witness's identification is unreliable. If the court concludes that the testimony is reliable, it will be admitted despite the suggestiveness of the procedures. Courts consider the following five factors in evaluating this: (1) whether the witness had an adequate opportunity to view the suspect at the time of the crime, (2) the witness's degree

of attention, (3) the accuracy of the witness's prior description of the suspect, (4) the level of certainty exhibited at the time of the identification, and (5) the length of time between the crime and the identification. The premise underlying the relevance of these factors is that people who have sharp and clear memory impressions of an event are less vulnerable to suggestion. Consequently, the greater the witness's observation time and degree of attention at the time of the crime, the more accurate the witness's prior description, the higher the witness's level of certainty at the time of the identification, and the shorter the interval between the crime and the identification, the more likely it is that a court will admit evidence of a positive eyewitness identification despite suggestiveness of the identification procedure.

    a.   *United States v. Downs*—Part II

  3. A witness who has been exposed to an unnecessarily suggestive identification procedure under circumstances that create a substantial risk of misidentification will also be barred from making an identification of the defendant in the courtroom during the trial unless the judge concludes that the witness's testimony stems from independent recollection acquired at the time of the crime and not from having observed the accused at the suggestive pretrial identification procedure. The amount of time the witness was in the presence of the defendant; the distance between them; the lighting conditions; the witness's degree of attention to the defendant; the accuracy of any prior description of the perpetrator by the witness; the witness's level of certainty at the pretrial identification; and the length of time between the crime and the tainted identification are among the factors the judge will consider in deciding this.

§ 8.10   Right to Counsel During Pretrial Identification Procedures

  A. The Sixth Amendment right to counsel bars admission of evidence of pretrial identifications made during a critical stage lineup or showup unless counsel is present or the defendant makes a valid waiver.

    1. The "critical stage" concept encompasses lineups and showups conducted *after* the initiation of adversary criminal proceedings. Counsel's presence is needed during lineups and showups so that counsel can observe the procedure and be in a position to challenge admission of witness identification testimony at the trial if the procedure is conducted in an unnecessarily suggestive manner that created a substantial likelihood of misidentification.

    2. The "critical stage" concept does not apply to:

      a. Lineups and showups conducted before the initiation of adversary judicial proceedings.

b. Photographic identification procedures, whether conducted before or after prosecution is commenced, because (1) the defendant is not present during the procedure and (2) counsel's presence as an observer is not necessary to enable counsel to challenge the procedure as impermissibly suggestive because the photographic spread can be reassembled for counsel to see.

B. Before conducting a critical stage lineup or showup, police must advise the defendant of the right to counsel and secure a waiver or wait until counsel is present.

C. A witness who makes a pretrial identification that is inadmissible on Sixth Amendment grounds will be barred from making a courtroom identification during the trial unless the prosecution proves by clear and convincing evidence that the witness's courtroom testimony is based on independent recall.

Review Questions

1. What functions does the Sixth Amendment right to counsel serve in our adversary system of criminal justice? (§ 8.1)

2. For what crimes do indigent defendants have the right to appointment of counsel? (§ 8.2)

3. What three requirements are necessary for a pretrial event to be considered a "critical stage" in a criminal prosecution? (§ 8.3(A))

4. When is a criminal prosecution considered to have been initiated? (§ 8.10(A))

5. When, if ever, must a court appoint counsel before compelling an indigent defendant to appear in a pretrial lineup? Before showing the defendant's photograph to an eyewitness? Discuss. (§§ 8.3, 8.10)

6. List all pretrial court appearances and investigative encounters that the Supreme Court has held to be critical stages in a criminal prosecution for purposes of the Sixth Amendment right to counsel. (§ 8.3)

7. When, if ever, is a suspect entitled to have counsel present during police investigative procedures conducted *prior* to the formal initiation of a criminal prosecution? During what procedures? (§ 8.3)

8. What inquiries must a trial judge make before allowing a criminal defendant to waive the right to counsel and represent him- or herself at the trial? (§ 8.4)

9. What must a defendant establish in order to have his or her conviction overturned on the basis of ineffective assistance of counsel? (§ 8.5)

10. After adversary judicial proceedings have commenced, police must either secure a valid waiver of the Sixth Amendment right to counsel or wait until counsel is present before conducting a lineup, showup, or police-initiated interrogation. What action must the police take to obtain a valid waiver of the Sixth Amendment right to counsel from: (a) A criminal defendant who has already retained counsel? (b) A criminal defendant who has not yet retained or requested appointment of counsel? (C) A juvenile? (§ 8.6)

11. Police use three different kinds of pretrial identification procedures. Identify and describe them. (§ 8.7)

12. Four constitutional provisions apply to pretrial identifications. Identify them. (§ 8.7)

13. What identification procedures may be used after a lawful custodial arrest? After a lawful investigatory detention? (§ 8.8)

14. Which of the following witness identifications is subject to suppression from the Fourth Amendment exclusionary rule? (§ 8.7)
    a.   Police arrest Sam without probable cause and compel him to participate in a lineup. An eyewitness identifies him.
    b.   Police arrest Sam without probable cause and take him to the crime scene for a show-up identification. An eyewitness identifies him.
    c.   Police detain Sam for investigation without reasonable suspicion and photograph him. An eyewitness identifies him from the photograph.
    d.   Police detain Sam for investigation based on reasonable suspicion and compel him to accompany them to the police station for a lineup. A witness identifies him.

15. What standard is used to determine when pretrial identification testimony is inadmissible under the due process clause? (§ 8.9)

16. Which of the three witness identification procedures can be challenged under the due process clause? (§ 8.9)

17. There are two ways in which unnecessary suggestiveness can be injected into a pretrial witness identification. What are they? (§ 8.9)

18. Which of the three witness identification procedures is the most suggestive? (§ 8.9)

19. When is it appropriate for the police to use a show-up identification? (§ 8.9)

20. When is it appropriate for the police to suggest to the witness whom to pick during a witness identification procedure? (§ 8.9)

21. What factors do courts consider in determining whether the witness's pretrial identification is sufficiently reliable to be admitted into evidence despite the suggestiveness of the identification procedure? (§ 8.9)

22. When does a suspect have a Sixth Amendment right to have counsel present during a witness identification procedure?

Chapter 9
Trial and Punishment

Objectives

This chapter examines the constitutional safeguards in effect during the trial and punishment phases of a criminal case. These safeguards include:

1.   Protection against double jeopardy.

2.   The right to a speedy trial.

3.   The right to a public trial.

4.   The right to confront adverse witnesses.

5.   The right to a fair trial before an impartial tribunal.

6.   The right to trial by jury.

7.   Protection against cruel and unusual punishment.

Discussion Outline

§9.1   Overview of Constitutional Safeguards during the Trial and Punishment Phases of a Criminal Case

§9.2   The Fifth Amendment Double Jeopardy Prohibition

      A.   The double jeopardy clause of the Fifth Amendment declares that no person "shall . . . be subject for the same offense to be twice placed in jeopardy of life or limb . . ."

      B.   The policy behind this safeguard is to prevent the government from using its vast resources to repeatedly retry an accused until he or she is too exhausted, psychologically and financially, to put forth an adequate defense.

C. The ban on double jeopardy imposes two closely related restrictions on the government.

    1. It prevents the government from trying an accused more than once for the same offense.

    2. It also prevents the government from imposing more than one punishment for the same offense.

§9.3   Prohibition of Multiple Prosecutions for the Same Offense

A. Ingredients necessary for protection against reprosecution. Three ingredients are neces-sary for a defendant to have double jeopardy protection against a second prosecution:

    1. An earlier prosecution must progress to the point of jeopardy attachment;

    2. The subsequent prosecution must involve the "same offense"; and

    3. Both prosecutions must be brought by the same government entity.

B. Jeopardy attachment. Jeopardy attaches in jury trials when the jury is empaneled, and in bench trials when the first witness has been sworn and the judge begins taking testimony. Once a criminal prosecution progresses to the jeopardy attachment point, the accused cannot be retried for the same offense by the same sovereign entity unless:

    1. The defendant requests a dismissal or mistrial before a verdict is reached;

    2. The judge grants a mistrial for reasons of manifest necessity, such as a deadlocked jury; or

    3. The defendant is convicted, appeals, and the conviction is overturned. However, retrial is foreclosed when a conviction is reversed based on a finding that the evidence presented at the first trial was legally insufficient to support a conviction.

C. Same offense. When an accused is retried on different statutory charges, the court must decide whether the new charge represents the "same offense." The following tests are used:

    1. The "same elements" test treats successive criminal prosecutions under two different sections of the penal code as brought for the same offense, unless each statute violated requires proof of at least one distinct element. If each statute violated requires proof of at least one distinct element, the violations will be considered distinct offenses and the second prosecution may go forward even though both charges

are based on the same underlying conduct. The "same elements" test is required in federal courts and is used by most state courts.

    2.   The "same transaction" test measures the number of offenses by the underlying conduct. All statutory violations occasioned by the same underlying conduct must be joined together for prosecution at a single trial. The "same transaction" test is used in only a few jurisdictions.

    D.   Same sovereign entity. The double jeopardy bar applies only if the *same* government attempts to reprosecute the *same* person for the *same* offence. It does not prevent successive prosecutions of the same person for the same offense by different sovereign entities when the offense is a crime against both.

§9.4   Prohibition of Multiple Punishments for the Same Offense

    A.   The double jeopardy clause also prohibits more than one punishment for the same offense. The concept of punishment does not include civil sanctions. The Fifth Amendment does not prohibit the government from enforcing civil and criminal sanctions for the same offense.

    1.   Whether a sanction is criminal or civil depends on whether the legislature sought to further a punitive or nonpunitive goal. If the legislature sought to further a nonpunitive goal, the sanction will be classified as civil and double jeopardy protection against multiple punishments for the same offense will be denied.

§9.5   Sixth Amendment and Due Process Requirements for Fair Trials

    A.   The Sixth Amendment and due process requirements for a fair trial include the guarantee of a speedy and public trial; the requirement that the tribunal assembled to pass judgment on the accused be impartial; the right to trial by jury; and the right to confront and cross-examine adverse witnesses.

§9.6   Speedy Trial

    A.   The right to a speedy trial is guaranteed by the Sixth Amendment.

    B.   This guarantee is designed to protect the accused from lengthy pretrial incarcerations, prolonged anxiety and concern, and erosion of evidence needed to defend against the charges.

    C.   The right to a speedy trial attaches when the suspect becomes an "accused" through an indictment, information, or similar method of initiating formal charges. Delays before a suspect has been formally charged with a crime are not taken into account in determining whether the right to a speedy trial has been denied.

D. Courts consider the following factors in assessing whether the right to a speedy trial has been denied: (1) the length of the delay, (2) the reasons for the delay, (3) whether the defendant made a timely assertion of his or her right to a speedy trial or sat idly by, and (4) whether the defendant was prejudiced by the government's delay in trying him or her.

§9.7   Public Trial

A. The right to a public trial is guaranteed by the Sixth Amendment.

B. Public trials are considered important for the following three reasons: (1) witnesses are more likely to tell the truth when they are required to testify in front of an audience; (2) unknown persons with information about the crime may learn about the trial and be induced to come forward; and (3) public trials afford citizens an opportunity to observe the proceedings and contribute to the perception that justice has been done.

C. The guarantee of a public trial applies both to the actual trial and to ancillary pretrial proceedings, like voir dire examinations of potential jurors, and hearings on motions to suppress illegally seized evidence.

1. Trial judges have the power to close the courtroom to public access only in urgent circumstances when exclusion of the public is necessary to serve higher values. The trial judge must consider alternatives before taking this action and must make findings adequate to support it.

2. Grand jury proceedings are an exception to the guarantee of a public trial. Grand jury proceedings are conducted in secret.

D. Members of the media and the public have a complementary right to attend criminal trials; the right of the media and the public is grounded in the common law and the First Amendment. (The media's right to attend criminal trials is covered in §9.10(C) of this outline.)

§9.8   Confrontation of Adverse Witnesses

A. The Sixth Amendment confrontation clause guarantees the accused the right to be present during the trial, to face prosecution witnesses who testify against him or her, and to cross-examine them in open court.

1. The accused may forfeit his or her right to be present during the trial by failing to show up for the trial or by being so disruptive that it is necessary to remove him or her from the courtroom.

2. The accused's right to confront prosecution witnesses face-to-face in open court may, in rare cases, be subordinated to the needs of child witnesses. In *Maryland v. Craig*, the Supreme Court ruled that trial judges may permit child witnesses to testify via one-way

closed-circuit television, but only on a case-specific finding that the particular witness would suffer such severe distress at testifying in the defendant's presence as to be incapable of communicating.

§9.9   Fair and Impartial Tribunal

A. The Sixth Amendment guarantees the accused the right to have his or her guilt determined by an impartial jury; the Fourteenth Amendment due process clause embodies a similar guarantee for bench trials.

B. Impartiality means that the decisionmaker (i.e., jurors or judge)

   1. Has no personal stake in the outcome;

   2. Harbors no personal animosity toward the accused;

   3. Is able to set aside prejudice against any class to which the defendant belongs;

   4. Is able to set aside any preconceived notions about the proper outcome of the case and to render a verdict based solely on the evidence presented at trial.

§9.10   Pretrial Publicity

A. The due process standard for whether jurors who have been exposed to prejudicial media coverage can render an impartial verdict is whether they can set aside their impressions and render a verdict based on evidence presented in court.

   1. Courts consider the following factors in applying this standard: (1) the prejudicial nature of the disclosures, (2) the extent of publicity, (3) the proximity to the time of trial, (4) the attitudes revealed by jurors during their voir dire examination.

B. Precautions traditionally used to counteract the effects of prejudicial media coverage include: (1) making special efforts to identify and eliminate prospective jurors with fixed opinions about the defendant's guilt during voir dire; (2) postponing the trial until the case has lost its notoriety; (3) changing the venue of the trial to a different community, and (4) sequestering jurors during the trial.

C. Trial judges occasionally use more radical measures to keep prejudicial disclosures out of print. Some measures have been held to violate the First Amendment.

   1. Orders directing media representatives not to publish lawfully obtained information are unconstitutional.

2. Orders closing courtroom proceedings while the trial is in session are of questionable constitutionality.

3. Orders closing pretrial suppression hearings are constitutional under the conditions stated in *Gannett Co. v. DePasquale*.

4. Orders directing attorneys, witnesses, and law enforcement officers to refrain from making extrajudicial comments about specified aspects of the case are constitutional.

§9.11   Trial by Jury

A. The right to trial by jury is guaranteed by the Sixth Amendment, made applicable to the states through the Fourteenth Amendment due process clause.

B. The Sixth Amendment right to trial by jury is available in all criminal cases except the trial of: (1) petty offenses (defined for Sixth Amendment jury trial purposes as crimes carrying a maximum punishment of six months' incarceration); (2) criminal contempt charges in which the judge imposes a sentence of incarceration of no more than six months; (3) military proceedings; (4) juvenile court proceedings, and (5) sentencing proceedings.

C. The common law trial jury (i.e., petit jury) consisted of 12 individuals.

1. This feature continues to be constitutionally required in federal criminal prosecutions and is used in a majority of state courts.

2. States are free to reduce the size of trial juries, but not below six in felony trials.

D. The Sixth Amendment mandates unanimous verdicts in federal criminal prosecutions, but permits less-than-unanimous verdicts in state criminal prosecutions. *Apodaca v. Oregon*.

E. The Sixth Amendment requires that juries be drawn from a source fairly representative of a cross section of the community in which the trial is held.

1. Systematic exclusion from jury rolls of members of any distinctive group violates the Constitution.

2. The prosecutor's use of peremptory challenges to strike potential jurors solely because of their race or gender also violates the Constitution.

§9.12   Preservation and Disclosure of Evidence Favorable to the Defense

    A.   A defendant's due process right to a fair trial is violated, entitling the defendant to a new trial, when the prosecutor or police:

        1.   violate the disclosure requirement established in *Brady v. Maryland*, 373 U.S. 83, 83 S. Ct. 1194, 10 L. Ed. 2d 215 (1963).

        2.   fail to preserve evidence under the conditions stated in *Arizona v. Youngblood*, 488 U.S. 51, 109 S. Ct. 333, 102 L. Ed. 2d 281 (1988).

    B.   *Brady* disclosure requirement. The prosecutor has a duty under the due process clause to disclose to the accused: (1) all evidence in the *prosecutor's possession or control* that is (2) *favorable* to the defendant and (3) *material* to guilt or the sentence. This duty applies irrespective of the prosecutor's good faith or bad faith and whether or not the defense requests the evidence.

    C.   *Arizona v. Youngblood* duty to preserve evidence. The *Youngblood* rule applies when government fails to preserve evidence that the defendant later claims would have been useful to him or her at trial. In order for the failure to preserve evidence to violate due process, three conditions are necessary: (1) the exculpatory value of the evidence must be apparent to the police before its destruction; (2) the nature of the evidence must be such that the defendant would be unable to obtain comparable evidence by other reasonably available means; and (3) the police must act in bad faith in failing to preserve the evidence.

§§9.13-9.15   The Eighth Amendment Protection against Cruel and Unusual Punishment

The Eighth Amendment prohibits excessive fines and cruel and unusual punishments, and has been interpreted to provide the following protections:

    A.   The Eighth Amendment limits the kinds of punishments for a crime to fines, victim restitution, prison terms, and executions carried out in a humane fashion.

    B.   Death is the most severe penalty that any society can impose. The Eighth Amendment places the following limitations on imposition of the death penalty:

        1.   The death penalty may not be imposed for any crime that does not involve the taking of a human life. *Coker v. Georgia*—Part II.

        2.   Legislatures may not make the death penalty mandatory, even for the most heinous crimes; discretion to impose this sentence is necessary.

3. Death penalty sentencing discretion must be channeled and focused by establishing statutory aggravating factors that must be present to warrant imposition of the death penalty.

4. Defendants facing the death penalty must be afforded an unrestricted opportunity to offer mitigating evidence that might convince the tribunal to show mercy.

5. The guilt and sentencing phases of a capital punishment case must be tried separately.

6. The death penalty may not be imposed on minors under age 18, the mentally retarded, or the criminally insane.

C. The Eighth Amendment imposes two restrictions on prison officials. They must:

1. Refrain from unnecessary and sadistic applications of force, and

2. Provide for a prisoner's "basic human needs."

     a. Prison officials are liable for failing to provide for a prisoner's basic needs only when they are actually aware that these needs are not being met and act with deliberate indifference.

Review Questions

1. Which constitutional amendment prohibits placing an accused twice in jeopardy for the same offense? (§9.2)

2. What policy does the double jeopardy restraint promote? (§9.2)

3. What three conditions must exist for a defendant to have double jeopardy protection against a second prosecution? (§9.3)

4. When does jeopardy attach in a jury trial? In a bench trial? (§9.3)

5. Identify the three situations in which the same sovereign entity may reprosecute a defendant for the same offense after an earlier prosecution progresses beyond the jeopardy attachment point? (§9.3)

6. In *United States v. Perez*, the Supreme Court enunciated the "manifest necessity" exception to the double jeopardy prohibition. What is the manifest necessity exception? Give examples of cases in which this exception applies. (§9.3)

7. Under what circumstances may the same government entity retry an accused for the same offense after an acquittal? (§9.3)

8. Under what circumstances may the same government entity retry an accused for the same offense following a conviction? (§9.3)

9. Two tests are used to determine whether charges brought under different portions of the penal code represent the "same offense." What are they? What standard does each test use to determine offense identity? Which test is most prevalent? (§9.3)

10. The double jeopardy clause also prohibits multiple punishments for the same offense. How do courts determine whether laws that disadvantage offenders beyond their initial punishment exact a second "punishment" for the same offense or impose a civil sanction? (§9.4)

11. Do the following constitute punishments or civil sanctions? (1) Laws authorizing the government to seize money or property gained from or used in connection with criminal activity; (2) "Megan's" laws, requiring convicted sexual offenders to register with local law enforcement authorities upon taking up residence in the county; (3) Sexual predator laws requiring the involuntary civil commitment of habitual sexual offenders after completion of their prison sentence. (§9.4)

12. Which amendment guarantees the right to a speedy trial? (§9.6)

13. What policies does the right to a speedy trial promote? (§9.6)

14. At what point in the criminal process does the right to a speedy trial attach? (§9.6)

15. What legal protection, if any, is available to a defendant against inordinate delays in arresting or charging him or her? (§9.6)

16. What factors do courts consider in determining whether the right to a speedy trial has been denied? (§9.6)

17. Which amendment guarantees the right to a public trial? (§9.7)

18. Why are public trials considered important? (§9.7)

19. Does the guarantee of a public trial apply to pretrial proceedings? Grand jury proceedings? (§9.7)

20. Under what circumstances, if any, may a trial judge exclude media representatives and the public from pretrial and trial proceedings without violating the defendant's right to a public trial? (§9.7)

21. Define the following terms: *grand jury*, *petit jury*, and *voir dire*. (§9.7 & Glossary)

22. Which amendment guarantees the accused the right to confront adverse witnesses? (§9.8)

23. What does "confrontation of adverse witnesses" involve? (§9.8)

24. Are there any circumstances in which a defendant may be denied the right to a face-to-face confrontation with a witness who testifies against him or her? (§9.8)

25. What four attributes must the decisionmaker possess in order to be considered impartial? (§ 9.9)

26. What standard is used to determine whether jurors who have been exposed to prejudicial media coverage can render an impartial verdict? (§9.10)

27. What factors do courts consider in applying this standard? (§9.10)

28. What three precautions have trial judges traditionally taken to counteract the effects of prejudicial media coverage? What are their shortcomings? (§9.10)

29. Define the term *sequester*. (§9.10 & Glossary)

30. Under what circumstances, if any, may a criminal trial judge:
    a. order media representatives to withhold publication of information already in the hands of the media?
    b. bar media representatives from attending criminal trials?
    c. bar media representatives and members of the public from attending pretrial suppression hearings?
    d. order attorneys, witnesses, and law enforcement officers to abstain from making extrajudicial comments about specific aspects of the case?

31. The *ABA Standards on Fair Trial and Free Press* establish guidelines on the pretrial release of information concerning pending criminal cases. What subjects are appropriate matters for public comment? What subjects are inappropriate? (§9.10; Part II)

32. Which constitutional amendment guarantees the right to trial by jury? (§9.11)

33. There are five criminal proceedings or portions thereof in which the defendant does not have a right to trial by jury. What are they? (§9.11)

34. The common law petit jury consisted of a panel of 12 individuals whose verdict had to be unanimous. Does the Sixth Amendment permit the federal government to use smaller petit juries? How small? To eliminate the requirement that the verdict be unanimous? Does the Sixth Amendment allow states to use smaller petit juries? How small? To eliminate the requirement that verdicts be unanimous? (§9.11)

35. Which constitutional amendment is the source of the prosecutor's *Brady* duty to disclose evidence to the defense? (§9.12)

36. What three elements must the defendant prove in order to establish that the prosecutor violated the *Brady* duty to disclose? Is it necessary for the defendant to prove that his or her attorney requested disclosure? That the prosecutor was personally aware of the existence of the suppressed evidence? That the prosecutor acted in bad faith? (§9.12)

37. When is evidence considered to be in the "prosecutor's possession and control" for *Brady* purposes? (§9.12)

38. When is evidence considered "favorable" for *Brady* purposes? Give several examples. (§9.12)

39. What three elements must a defendant prove in order to establish a police violation of the *Arizona v. Youngblood* duty to preserve evidence? (§9.12 & *Arizona v. Youngblood* (Part II))

40. Which amendment prohibits cruel and unusual punishment? (§9.13)

41. What four kinds of punishments, commonplace in modern society, are considered to be neither cruel nor unusual? (§9.13)

42. For what crimes is the death penalty regarded as unconstitutionally cruel punishment? (§9.14)

43. What case marked the beginning of the Supreme Court's capital punishment sentencing reforms? What did this case hold? (§9.14)

44. The Eighth Amendment has been interpreted to require death penalty sentencing procedures to incorporate certain safeguards. What safeguards are necessary? (§9.14)

45. For what crimes may the death penalty be made mandatory? (§9.14)

46. What three classes of offenders are not death-penalty eligible? (§9.14)

47. The Eighth Amendment prohibition on cruel and unusual punishment imposes two categories of duties on prison officials. What are they? (§9.15)

48. What must a prison inmate establish to assert a claim against a correctional officer for using excessive force? (§9.16)

49. What must a prison inmate establish to assert a claim against prison officials for failing to provide for his or her welfare? (§9.16)

Chapter 10

Constitutional Rights and Liabilities in the Workplace

Objectives

Many students who read this book will someday be police officers. This chapter examines the constitutional rights of officers in personnel disputes, federal protection against employment discrimination, and civil liability for violating the constitutional rights of others. The student should emerge from this chapter with a clear understanding of:

1. First Amendment protection for on- and off-duty speech;

2. Fourth Amendment protection against workplace searches for evidence of work-related misconduct;

3. Fifth Amendment protection against compulsory self-incrimination during police internal investigations;

4. Fourteenth Amendment procedural rights in police disciplinary actions;

5. Fourteenth Amendment protection against department regulations that arbitrarily infringe on a police officer's personal liberty; and

6. Title VII protection against employment discrimination based on race, creed, color, religion, gender, and nation origin.

7. Civil liability under 42 U.S.C. § 1983 for violating the constitutional rights of others.

Discussion Outline

§10.1   Introduction

    A. The constitutional rights studied in earlier chapters have a narrower application in the workplace. Officers retain constitutional rights only to the extent that their exercise is compatible with the police department's fulfillment of its service obligations to the public.

§10.2   First Amendment Protection for Work-Related Speech

Police officers are entitled to First Amendment protection for speech that antagonizes superiors only when: (1) they speak in their capacity as a citizen (as opposed to as an employee), (2) about a matter of public (as opposed to private) concern, and (3) the importance of their speech outweighs its potential to cause a disruption in the workplace.

    A. Speech as a Citizen

        1. Police officers have two personas. They are both citizens and public employees. When they perform speech tasks required by their job, they speak in their capacity as an employee and have no First Amendment protection. This limitation derives from *Garcetti v. Ceballos*—Part II.

        2. The Garcetti case does not completely eliminate First Amendment protection for on-the-job speech. The citizen/employee nature of the speech turns on whether it arose out of the performance of the speaker's job responsibilities. If it did, the inquiry is over; the employee loses no matter how important the information is to the public's evaluation of the performance of the agency where the employee works. If it did not, then the court will go on to the second question: Did the speech relate to a matter of public or private concern?

        3. Speech the arises out of the officer's professional responsibilities is not transformed into the speech of a citizen by going public and sharing it with the media.

        Andrew v. Clark—Part II.

    B. Matter of "public concern."

        1. The topic must be some of interest persons outside the department, and

        2. The officer must be motivated to speak, at least in part, to promote interests beyond his or her own.

        a.   Speech that relates to an officer's private concerns in matters like work assignments, personnel actions, promotions, internal grievances, and the like carries no First Amendment protection.

        b.   *Connick v. Myers*—Part II.

C.   Balancing the officer's interest against the interest of the department.

If the officer's claim survives the first two inquiries, the court will determine whether disciplinary action was justified by weighing the importance of the officer's speech against its potential for disruptiveness.

    1.   Because police departments have a greater need to maintain loyalty, discipline, and respect for authority than the typical government employer, the department's decision to impose discipline will generally be upheld if the officer's speech caused a disturbance in the workplace unless the speech addressed a matter of unusually strong public concern.

D.   Off-duty speech away from the workplace on subjects unrelated to the officer's employment is more likely to be protected because the officer is now speaking as a citizen. However, discipline is justified even for off-duty speech when the speech has a negative effect on the police department.

    1.   *Locurto v. Giuliani*—Part II.

E.   The First Amendment prohibits government agencies from discharging employees because of their party affiliation unless the job is a "policy-making position" in which the employee acts as an advisor or spokesperson for an elected public official or is privy to confidential information, making party loyalty and shared ideological beliefs an appropriate requirement for the job.

§10.3   Fourth Amendment Protection against Workplace Searches

A.   To challenge a workplace search conducted as part of an internal investigation: (1) an officer must have a reasonable expectation of privacy in the location searched, *and* (2) the search must be conducted without reasonable suspicion of job-related misconduct.

    1.   No Fourth Amendment privacy interest exists in an officer's squad car, desk, locker, or other department property issued for official use unless the officer has been given exclusive dominion and control and no one else has access to it. The department's reservation of an unlimited right of inspection also precludes the existence of a reasonable expectation of privacy.

2. Even with a reasonable expectation of privacy, a workplace search is permitted whenever the department has reasonable suspicion that the search will turn up evidence that the officer is guilty of work-related misconduct. Probable cause and a search warrant are not necessary.

     a. *Ortega v. O'Connor*—Part II.

     b. *People v. Neal*—Part II.

B. Compulsory production of a urine sample for drug testing constitutes a search. Police officers may be forced to undergo drug testing only when: (1) the department has reasonable suspicion that they are abusing drugs, or (2) the testing is done pursuant to a systematic drug screening program.

     1. *National Treasury Employees Union v. Von Raab*—Part II.

§10.4   Fifth Amendment Privilege against Self-incrimination

A. Police officers undergoing an internal affairs investigation may be compelled to answer questions about their job performance and may be terminated for refusing, even though the answers are self-incriminating, because immunity arises by operation of law when a statement is compelled under threat of removal from office. This immunity is called *Garrity* immunity. *Garrity* immunity precludes use in a subsequent criminal prosecution of statements obtained under threat of removal from office; the department is limited to making disciplinary use of such statements.

     1. *Linger v. Fechko*—Part II.

§10.5   Fourteenth Amendment Protection for a Police Officer's Personal Liberty

A. Police officers are more heavily regulated than any government employees outside the military. Police department regulations that infringe on an officer's liberty outside the workplace are usually challenged on the theory that they violate substantive due process. This theory requires proof that the regulation had no rational relationship to *any* legitimate interest of the police department. Because police departments are looked upon as "paramilitary organizations," this theory rarely succeeds.

     1. Regulations affecting grooming, personal appearance, and obesity have all been upheld as constitutional.

         a. *Kelly v. Johnson*—Part II.

     2. The following regulations have also been upheld as constitutional: requiring police officers to be citizens of the United States, requiring police officers to reside in the political subdivision in which they are employed, prohibiting outside employment, and prohibiting smoking, either on or off the job.

3. Police officers may be disciplined for off-duty sexual behavior when the behavior has an adverse effect on the department.

§10.6   Procedural Due Process in Police Disciplinary Actions

The Fourteenth Amendment due process clause entitles police officers to notice of the charges and a hearing before the department may deprive them of a "property" or "liberty" interest.

A. *Procedural protection for officers with a property right in their job.* The Fourteenth Amendment due process clause entitles officers who have a property right in their job (i.e., who cannot be dismissed without just cause) to a hearing to contest whether grounds exit for a termination, demotion, or suspension. The protection afforded must, at minimum, include: (1) notice of the charges; (2) a hearing before an impartial decisionmaker; (3) an opportunity to challenge the department's evidence; and (4) an opportunity to present testimony.

B. *Procedural protection for probationary officers and others who lack a property right in their job.* Although probationary officers lack a property right in their job, they have a "liberty interest" in pursuing their chosen profession. They are entitled to a name-clearing hearing if they are dismissed based on stigmatizing charges disclosed to the public that could foreclose their ability to obtain other employment in law enforcement. A name-clearing hearing is a limited remedy. The purpose of the hearing is to refute the charges and clear their record, not to get their job back.

§10.7   Employment Discrimination Based on Race, Color, Religion, Gender, or National Origin

A. Title VII of the Civil Rights Act of 1964 makes it an unlawful employment practice for a police department to refuse to hire, discharge, or otherwise discriminate against any person because of the person's race, color, religion, gender, or national origin.

B. Title VII recognizes three kinds of VII discrimination claims: (1) disparate treatment, (2) disparate impact, and (3) sexual/racial harassment.

1. Disparate treatment discrimination occurs when one person is deliberately treated less favorably than others similarly situated because of the person's race, color, religion, gender, or national origin.

2. Disparate impact discrimination occurs when a police department uses selection criteria that disproportionately eliminate members of a protected class without being valid predictors of the knowledge, skills, or other traits necessary for the job.

a. *Dothard v. Rawlinson*—Part II.

3. Sexual/racial harassment.

    a. *Sexual Harassment.* Two basic forms of sexual harassment are recognized:

        i. *Quid pro quo sexual harassment* occurs when a superior threatens to take a negative action or to withhold a positive action unless the subordinate acquiesces in sexual demands.

        ii. *Hostile work environment sexual harassment* occurs when unwelcome verbal or physical conduct of a sexual nature is so severe or pervasive that it alters the conditions of the victim's employment and creates an intimidating, hostile, or abusive work environment:

        iii. *Persons liable.* Title VII imposes liability on employees who commit sexual harassment. Their employers can also be sued when: (1) the harassment is committed by a supervisor and the victim suffers tangible employment injury or (2) in the case of co-worker sexual harassment, the harasser's supervisor was aware that the harassment was taking place and did nothing to stop it.

    b. Hostile work environment harassment claims can also be brought by employees who are victims of racial, religious, and ethnic harassment when the harassment is sufficiently severe or pervasive as to create an intimidating, hostile, or abusive working environment.

§10.8   Equal Protection in the Police Workplace

The equal protection clause allows a police department to treat women and minorities more favorably in awarding jobs and promotions only when:

A. The treatment is necessary to eradicate the present effects of the department's own past discriminatory employment practices or to further the department's operational needs for diversity, *and*

B. The plan to address the department's needs is narrowly tailored to avoid causing unnecessary injury to those who are not beneficiaries.

C. Unless both requirements are satisfied, police department hiring and promotional policies that give more favorable treatment to women and minorities can be challenged as a denial of equal protection. Challenges brought on this theory are called reverse discrimination lawsuits.

§ 10.9   Constitutional Accountability under Federal Law

Police officers are civilly liable under § 1983 when (1) they act under color of state law, in (2) depriving an individual of a constitutional right.

A. *Under color of state law.* The Supreme Court has defined "action under color of state law" as referring to "the misuse of power, possessed by virtue of state law and made possible only because the wrongdoer is clothed with the authority of state law." A police officer's constitutional wrongs are treated as committed under "color of state law" in two situations: (1) the wrong occurs while undertaking official action, and (2) the wrong is committed for private gain under a false pretense of exercising legal authority. The first situation is more common.

   1. *Rogers v. City of Little Rock, Ark.*—Part II.

   2. Federal law enforcement agents cannot be sued under §1983 because they act under color of federal law. However, the Supreme Court has crafted an identical remedy for holding federal officials liable that arises directly under the Constitution.

B. *Deprivation of a constitutional right.* An officer's potential civil liability is coextensive with the entire Constitution and decisions interpreting it. Each time the Supreme Court announces a new constitutional ruling, it enlarges the decisional base on which § 1983 claims can be brought.

C. *Potential defendants in a § 1983 action.* Defendants in a § 1983 action are liable only for their own acts and omissions, not for what someone else did. The city, police department, and supervisory personnel can be held liable for a rank-and-file police officer's violation of the Constitution only if they did or failed to do something that caused the violation to occur, such as by not adequately training or supervising the offending officer. However, police officers who passively stand by and watch their comrades commit unlawful acts of violence are liable along with them, not for what their comrades did, but for what they failed to do. The Constitution imposes a duty on *them* to protect persons in custody against violence, including violence committed by their fellow officers.

   1. *Vann v. City of New York*—Part II.

   2. *Yang v. Hardin*—Part II.

D. *Qualified immunity.* Police officers make mistakes and errors of judgment just like anyone else. The defense of qualified immunity protects them from § 1983 liability if their conduct "does not violate clearly established statutory or constitutional rights of which a reasonable person would have known." Application of this test calls for two inquiries.

1. The first inquiry is whether the constitutional right the officer is charged with violating was clearly established at the time of the events that gave rise to the suit.

    a. To be "clearly established," the right must be established with sufficient clarity that a reasonable police officer should have been aware that the right existed, that it applied to this situation, and that his or her conduct violated it.

    b. This degree of clarity normally requires an authoritative precedent (i.e., a case decided by the U.S. Supreme Court, on-point case law decided by a federal court in the officer's own circuit, or a strong consensus of case law authority from other jurisdictions) applying the constitutional right to a factually similar case.

2. If the constitutional right was clearly established, the second inquiry is whether a reasonable police officer, confronted with the same facts, could have believed that the action taken complied with that standard.

Review Questions

1. Why do police officers have less constitutional protection in the workplace than the criminals they investigate? (§11.1)

2. Officer Dobosz was the first officer to arrive on the scene after a deadly shooting involving a teenager who had been shot in the back of the head by Officer Fitzgerald. He had to leave almost immediately after his arrival. When he returned, he noticed a knife near the dead boy's body that had not there when he left. Someone had planted the weapon there after the shooting so that Officer Fitzgerald could claim the shooting was justified by self-defense. Dobosz was deeply troubled by the incident, but kept the incident to himself for about a year. He contacted the FBI after learning that they were investigated the shooting. Officer Fitzgerald was placed on trial by the federal government. Dobosz testified at the trial that he believed that the killing of the youth was unnecessary and that the knife discovered near his body had been planted there. Officer Fitzgerald was acquitted. After the acquittal, the superintendent of police suspended Dobosz without pay. After his suspension was over, he was returned to duty, but his assignments were frequently changed, and he was constantly harassed. He sued, claiming a violation of his First Amendment rights.

    a. Describe the three-step process the court will use to determine whether Officer Dobosz's First Amendment rights were violated by the action taken against him in response to his testimony against a fellow officer.

    b. How should the first inquiry be resolved?

    c. How should the second inquiry be resolved?

d. What is the third inquiry? What kind of workplace disruption is the testimony of one police against a fellow officer during a criminal trial likely to cause? Should that court find the department's interest in avoiding these disruptions outweighed Officer Dobosz's First Amendment interest in testifying? (§10.2)

3. When, if ever, may a public employee's party affiliation be taken into consideration in hiring, transfer, promotion, or dismissal decisions? (§10.2)

4. What two factors must be present for a police officer to have Fourth Amendment protection against a workplace search conducted for evidence of work-related misconduct? (§10.3; *Ortega v. O'Connor*—Part II).

5. The Whosville Police Department maintains lockers for the use of its employees. Department regulations provide that: "Officers shall: (1) keep their lockers clean and orderly, (2) not store articles of evidence, confiscated materials, contraband, intoxicants or food in their lockers at any time, and (3) provide their commanding officer with a duplicate key. The regulations further provide that "Commanding Officers shall periodically inspect all lockers assigned to personnel under their command." At 8:00 A.M. on January 13, 1998, Captain McDougall discovered illegal drugs on top of a heating duct in the police locker room. When he made a similar discovery two hours later, Captain McDougall notified Internal Affairs and directed his subordinates to open and search all 350 lockers in the police locker room. Drugs were found in Officer Johnson's locker and he was dismissed. Does Officer Johnson have a claim against the Department for violating his Fourth Amendment rights? (§ 10.3; *People v. Neal*—Part II)

6. When may a police officer be compelled to undergo work-related drug testing? (§10.3; *National Treasury Employees Union v. Von Raab*—Part II).

7. Officer Johnson was ordered to appear before the Whosville Police Department internal affairs unit, which was investigating an allegation that he had taken a bribe. When he appears, he is ordered to cooperate and informed that if he fails to cooperate, he *will* be fired.
   a. Suppose Officer Johnson refuses to give a statement and is fired. Has the Whosville Police Department violated Officer Johnson's Fifth Amendment privilege against self-incrimination? Explain.
   b. Suppose Officer Johnson, fearful of losing his job, admits to taking bribe. May his admission be used as evidence against him in a subsequent criminal proceeding? Explain. (§ 10.4)

8. What must a police officer establish in order to successfully challenge a police department regulation as a violation of substantive due process? (§10.5; *Kelly v. Johnson*—Part II)

9. How successful have police officers been in challenging police department regulations affecting:
   a. Grooming, personal appearance, and obesity?

    b.   *Minimum* height and weight requirements?

    c.   Citizenship requirements?

    d.   Residency requirements?

    e.   Bans on smoking?

    f.   Off-duty sexual behavior? (§10.5)

10. The Fourteenth Amendment due process clause entitles police officers facing adverse employment action to a hearing in certain instances.
    a. When is a police officer facing dismissal entitled to a hearing to contest grounds for his or her dismissal?
    b. What procedural safeguards must be provided at the hearing? (§10.6)
    c. What is a "name-clearing" hearing?
    d. When is a police officer entitled to a name-clearing hearing?

11. Title VII prohibits police departments from refusing to hire, discharging, or otherwise discriminating against people on any one of five different grounds. What are the five grounds? (§10.7)

12. Identify and describe the three kinds of discrimination claims that can be brought under Title VII. (§10.7)

13. What must a claimant prove in order to establish *quid pro quo* sexual harassment? Hostile workplace sexual harassment? (§10.7)

14. When is a police department liable for a supervisor's sexual harassment of a subordinate? A co-worker? (§10.7)

15. What are affirmative action programs? (§10.8)

16. Officer Johnson, a white male officer, had the highest score on the sergeant's promotional exam. The Whosville Police Department, nevertheless, passed over him and appointed Officer Ricardo, a Hispanic officer, who scored five points lower, based on the Department's affirmative action plan. Officer Johnson sued the Department, claiming he was denied equal protection of the laws. What two inquiries will the court make to decide whether the preferential treatment given to Officer Ricardo violated Officer Johnson's right to equal protection? (§10.8)

17. What two things must a plaintiff prove to make a recovery against a police officer under §1983? (§10.9)

18. Officer Green is violence-prone. Last week alone, he shot two people with his service revolver. Indicate whether he was acting "under color of state law" so as to be amendable to suit under §1983 during the shooting incidents. (§10.9)
    a. Officer Green, who had been dispatched to the scene of a burglary, shot the burglar in the back of the head as he attempted to flee.
    b. Officer Green shot his wife with his service revolver during a domestic dispute. He was still on duty and in uniform and had stopped at home to pick up his lunch.

19. When can a municipality be sued under §1983 for the unconstitutional acts of a rank-and-file police officer? (§10.9)

20. What is the defense of qualified immunity available in a §1983 action? (§10.9)

21. What test do courts use to determine whether a constitutional right has been established with sufficient clarity that an officer can be held liable for violating it? What degree of case law specificity is generally necessary to satisfy this test? (§10.9)